THE RELIGION OF
ANCIENT GREECE

THE RELIGION
OF
ANCIENT GREECE

An Outline

BY

THADDEUS ZIELINSKI

Translated
from the Polish
with the author's co-operation
by
GEORGE RAPALL NOYES

 BOOKS FOR LIBRARIES PRESS
FREEPORT, NEW YORK

First Published 1926
Reprinted 1970

STANDARD BOOK NUMBER:
8369-5222-7

LIBRARY OF CONGRESS CATALOG CARD NUMBER:
76-107838

PRINTED IN THE UNITED STATES OF AMERICA

NOTE

THE present translation has been reviewed by
the author, who has made many corrections and
who has supplied the refei ences to Greek and
Latin writers. I am also deeply indebted to
Professor Ivan M. Linforth of the University of
California, who has revised the entire text with
great care, suggesting numerous changes in
English idiom and giving assistance in matters
of classical scholarship. Professor M. I. Ros-
tovtzeff of Yale University and Professor G. C.
Fiske of the University of Wisconsin have aided
me in certain matters, and the readers of the
Clarendon Press have been of great assistance
during the printing of the volume. Professor
William Popper of the University of California
has given me counsel on a reference to the
Talmud. Finally, I am grateful to my wife for
work on the Index and for constant help and
advice in various other ways.

G. R. N.

TABLE OF CONTENTS

vii

I

INTRODUCTION

AMONG all the so-called ' pagan ' religions there is none with which our educated classes are so familiar, and of which at the same time they are so profoundly ignorant, as the religion of ancient Greece. The statement may seem paradoxical, but it is nevertheless true.

Popular acquaintance with that religion is a heritage from two epochs. In the first place, not to go farther back, it dates from the epoch of French classicism of the seventeenth century, with its cult of Greek mythology in poetry, in the plastic arts, and in the ' gallantry ' of all the social life of that period. Hence the popularity of the gods of Greece—generally under their Latin names, to be sure, in accordance with the usage of French classicism. As a matter of fact, they dispossessed in men's consciousness the Christian saints. A believing Christian of the educated class, for whom the names of the saints of the Church, even though they were mentioned with the greatest veneration, were only names, had very definite ideas about Zeus

(or Jove) and Hera (or Juno), about the stern
Pallas (or Minerva) and the dissolute Aphrodite
(or Venus), about the warlike Mars and the
cunning Mercury.

His ideas were definite, certainly ; but were
they correct ? That is the question. And one
must answer : No, absolutely incorrect. The
very popularity of Greek *mythology* was the most
potent barrier to the understanding of Greek
religion ; it was one of the principal causes of
the fact that men refused to take the Greek
religion, as such, seriously. The tone was set
by Ovid, the singer of Roman gallantry of the
epoch of Augustus, which was so closely akin in
its temper to the age of the French *roi soleil* ;
and in the gorgeous garden of his *Metamorphoses*
one could find any perfume that he might desire
—except that of religion. Think of the incor-
rigible seducer, Jove, of the jealous and quarrel-
some Juno, of Mercury, the master of thievish
tricks, of the coquette Venus, of the tipsy
Bacchus—what room is there for religion in
such material ?

This, I repeat, is our heritage from one epoch,
that of French classicism. Its injurious influence
was partially neutralized at the end of the
eighteenth and the beginning of the nineteenth
century, during the epoch of the so-called
neohumanism of Winckelmann, Goethe, and
Schiller. A reaction set in, but mainly on an
aesthetic foundation. The Zeus of Phidias,

even in those later humble reproductions which
were all that Winckelmann was acquainted with,
is at all events not the voluptuous magnate of
Ovid ; and Goethe had good cause to admire
the spouse of Zeus, the Hera ascribed to Polyclitus, in whom he felt a breath ' as of a poem
of Homer'. And yet this reaction, the most
eloquent expression of which was the ardent
hymn of Schiller in honour of *The Gods of Greece*,
was of an exclusively aesthetic character. The
ancient deities, revealing themselves in beauty,
were contrasted with the peculiarly spiritual
nature of Christianity ; and when Goethe in an
unforgettable scene represented his tortured
Gretchen in prayer before the Mater Dolorosa :

> Incline, O Maiden,
> Thou sorrow-laden,
> Thy gracious countenance upon my pain !—
>
> [Tr. TAYLOR]

it never even entered his mind that she was
really invoking the immediate successor of a
goddess of old times, the type of all women
who are in affliction, Demeter.

Only through exact studies of the ancient
world could Greek religion receive just appre-
ciation ; such studies were naturally pursued
in the mysteries of classical philology, the science
of the ancient world. Proper methods were not
found at once : some studies led the investigators astray ; others, though good in themselves,
nevertheless did not lead to the goal which we

have here in view. The ardour of the times of
Winckelmann, joined with the mysticism of
Swedenborg and Cagliostro, produced a brilliant
flowering of ancient Greek 'symbolism' (Sainte-
Croix, Creuzer), and this in turn called forth an
extreme reaction in the spirit of the obsolete
'enlightenment', after which men hesitated to
breathe a word of the grace conferred by
the Eleusinian mysteries. The relatively rich
material furnished by the study of the sacred
books of India and Iran raised in a pressing form
the question of the origin of Greek ideas about
the gods ; this was ordinarily answered by a
theory of physical monism, which had as its
point of departure the phenomena of light (the
'solar theory' of Max Müller and others) or of
the atmosphere (Forchhammer). But, not to
speak of indubitable errors and narrowness, it
is evident that the Greek religion, as such,
could only be obscured by all these interpreta-
tions. Even if it be true that the original
Pallas Athena was a thunder-cloud, as is very
likely, nevertheless such was not the nature of
that Athena who, according to the religious
conceptions of Solon, held over his country her
protecting arms and by her magnanimous inter-
cession saved it from destruction. It is evident
that the methods of the 'historical school',
which studied the development of cults in the
early epochs of the wanderings and crossings
of the Greek tribes, also failed to lead directly

to an explanation of the inner nature of the Greek
religion ; and if, notwithstanding this, the name
of the founder of the school, Otfried Müller,
must be mentioned with honour as that of one
of the chief hierophants of Hellenism, this is
because he managed to unite, both in his books
on the history of the Greek tribes and in his
edition of the *Eumenides* of Aeschylus, the genetic
aim of his work with service to the problem of
which we are now speaking.

Much light has now been thrown on these
matters ; among classical philologists a just
estimate of the religion of ancient Greece is an
accomplished fact. When—to mention only
two of its leading students—Erwin Rohde says
that both the deepest and the boldest thoughts
about divinity arose in ancient Greece, and when
Wilamowitz calls the Hellenes ' the most devout
nation of the world ', the nature of the transformation that has taken place in our views of
Greek religion becomes clear. And yet, in the
first place, this new conception has not yet
become generally known among educated
people ; and, in the second place, a detailed
portrayal of the Greek religion remains, as
before, a problem for the future. Naturally it
must rest on an historic foundation ; but
though works exist which proudly call themselves histories of Greek religion, they are at
best only good collections of materials. The
present writer has not lost hope that it may be

granted him to supply this pressing need ; the
spirit in which he plans to do so is shown by the
corresponding chapters in his short *History of
Ancient Culture*. His present problem is different : the historic point of view is set aside ;
the topic will be the *essence of Greek religion in
the flourishing epoch of the Greek people*.

But where shall we find this ' essence ' of the
Greek religion ?

The answer is beset with difficulties ; and in
these very difficulties lies the *internal cause* of
that lack of acquaintance of the educated classes
of Europe with the Greek religion of which
I have been speaking.

Where shall we find the essence of Christianity ?   In the Gospels.—The essence of
Judaism ?   In the Torah and the Prophets.—
The essence of Islam ?   In the Koran.   These
are all canonical books, every verse of which is
characteristic and authoritative in the opinion
of the adherents of these different religions.
Their rise was due to the existence of a founder
of a religion and of a powerful priesthood, which
maintained the real or fancied purity of its
teaching free from foreign ingredients.   These
two elements were lacking in the religion of
ancient Greece ; this fact constitutes its strength,
but at the same time its weakness.   The very
concept of a ' canon ' in this field was absolutely
foreign to the freedom-loving spirit of the Hellene.
Quite properly the Fathers of the Church called

Hellenism 'the father of all heresies'; the word 'heresy' means 'choice', and the right of choice was for a Hellene the inseparable mark of intellectual liberty. Of what sort is the 'nature' of the deity ? Is that being something purely spiritual, non-material ? Or is it merely woven of the most subtle, imperishable sub-stance, of the 'heavenly ether', and therefore not subject to change of material, not requiring food or drink or sleep ? Or finally, is it in general like man, except that it has in its veins not blood, but 'ichor', that it feeds not on bread but on nectar and ambrosia, and therefore does not grow old and does not die ? All these views were expressed ; every man could regard as correct the view which for him was most intelligible and congenial ; and any man would have become a laughing-stock if it had occurred to him to invoke the thunders of heaven and earth on the head of a person who thought and believed differently from himself. But, on the other hand, when the full moon of the month of Hekatom-baion shines in the heavens, then every Athenian will go forth into the streets, up to the Acropolis, that he may gaze on the solemn procession of old men, youths and maidens as it passes through the Propylaea to the temple of Athena of the Citadel ; his heart will throb with holy emotion at the notes of the ancient hymn in her honour—
'Hail to thee, dread goddess, amid the din of battle' (compare Aristophanes, *Clouds* 967)—and

happy will be the man who beholds his young daughter among the maidens carrying baskets to the goddess.

So there is no canonical book, or Bible, for the Hellenic religion. Neither is there any such rich theological literature as comes to the aid of the investigator of the religion of India, Egypt or Babylon. The absence of it, to be sure, is not organic, but accidental. Like other religions, that of Greece was revealed—that is, regarded itself as revealed ; it had its theophanies and its prophets. But the theophanies, in so far as they expressed themselves in the revelation of ceremonies and teachings, led to the establishment of secret, mystical cults, which became hereditary in the family of their elect founder. Thus Demeter revealed herself to the royal pair in Eleusis, Celeüs and Metanira, and her ' mysteries ' became hereditary in the line of the Eumolpidae—their secret was never disclosed. Of prophets ancient Greece knew not a few—I am thinking of prophets in the true sense of the word, not of soothsayers—from mythical times to the full bloom of the historical epoch : Melampus, Orpheus, Musaeus, Hesiod, Epimenides of Crete, Pythagoras, Empedocles, Diotima. And there existed a rich literature, in verse and prose, which proceeded directly or indirectly from them. But for us, alas, almost nothing of this literature has been preserved ; so we shall never find in it the essence of the Greek religion.

Where then ?

Everywhere—and therein lies the enormous difficulty of our problem.

First of all, in the whole of Greek *literature*, without exception : as a matter of fact there is not a single branch of it to which we do not owe some important evidence in the sphere of the questions that interest us. Literature, however, bears the stamp of the individuality of the authors who create it; therefore, that we may check its evidence by the point of view of the ' average Greek ', great importance attaches to *epigraphic evidence* : the edicts of communes in religious matters or matters bordering on religion, the expression of the religious feelings of common citizens on grave stones, votive offerings, and the like. And finally it is obvious that the *plastic tradition*—statues, bas-reliefs, wall-paintings and vase-paintings—is of first-rate importance for such a religion as the Greek ; one need only remember that this was what opened the eyes of Winckelmann and his disciples to that religion.

I have called enormous, the difficulty that results from this abundance of sources ; as a matter of fact, it lies not only in the necessity of mastering this wide-spread material, but also in the variety and inconsistency of the evidence gained from it. The Arcadian shepherds flogged with nettles the statue of their god Pan, if they were disappointed in their hopes of a treat from

the farmer for whom they worked : is that
' Greek religion ' ?   Most assuredly, seeing that
the Arcadians were Greeks.   Socrates prayed to
the gods to send him good, even if he should not
ask for it, and not to send him evil, even if he
should ask for it : is that also ' Greek religion ' ?
Evidently so, seeing that Socrates was a Greek.
And between these two poles what a many-
coloured rainbow of dark and light tints of religious feeling !   How shall we escape from being
blinded by this bewildering mixture of varied
shades ?

The ancients themselves propounded this
question and replied to it—in about the third
century before Christ—in the following manner.
Not one religion exists, but three, which are
binding in unequal measure.   In the first place,
poetic religion, otherwise called mythology.   It
binds no one ; and besides, every man by means
of allegorical interpretation may blend with his
religious consciousness, this or that branch of
it, and thereby transfer it to the sphere of the
second religion.   This religion is *philosophical*
religion.   It does not form a single whole : the
Academy understands the nature of the gods in
one way, the Lyceum in another, the Stoa in yet
a third, and Epicurus in a fashion widely different from all others.   Here also there is no
sort of binding obligation : every man, availing
himself of the right of choice (*hairesis*) that is
offered him, may follow the course that attracts

him and at the same time be free to go nowhere
at all, if nothing attracts him. The punishment
for an improper choice will be spiritual dissatis-
faction, the punishment for failure to choose
will be spiritual poverty; but a preacher would be
laughed to scorn if he should start to threaten
' dissenters ' with eternal tortures in the other
world. And finally there is a third religion, the
citizen's religion; this really binds the citizen,
as such. But it binds him only to share in the
cults of the state as a whole, not hampering his
conscience with any dogma—thus even here
there was no religious compulsion and oppression.
When he is elected archon, an Athenian citizen
on a certain day casts a pinch of incense on the
blazing altar of Artemis: on the part of a
religious man this act signified: ' I believe in
Artemis '; on the part of an unbeliever: ' I fulfil
the duty of an archon of the Athenian people '.
And one must call fanatic, not the man who in
the given conditions was obedient to the ancient
custom, but the man who could even think of
protesting against this innocent obedience.

As the reader sees, these three religions answer
more or less to what we now call the narrative, dogmatic, and ceremonial aspects of a
single religion. This is the reason why in the
present sketch we cannot restrict our field to
only one of them, even to the most binding of
the three, the citizen's religion: if we did, our
picture would be incomplete.

But since it is still less possible to include all the manifestations of the religious feelings of the Greeks in this short sketch, there is, I think, only one absolutely satisfactory solution of our problem. Let us transfer ourselves, believing Christians of the educated classes, into the Athens of the fifth and fourth centuries before Christ, and strive to answer this query : *What would be our own faith, if with our own souls and their needs we were living in those times ?* Obviously we should observe the festivals piously ordained by our fathers, and our magnanimous patroness aloft on the Acropolis would find in us her most ardent votaries ; we should be initiated into the blessed mysteries of Demeter of Eleusis with their profound teachings and with their ceremonies that exalt the spirit ; as schoolboys we should study thoroughly all of Homer, but of course we should never doubt that if Zeus threatens Hera with a beating, the meaning is only that the sky, clad in clouds, scourges with its thunders the expanse of the air ; regularly on the days of the Great Dionysia we should go to see the tragedies of our great poets, Aeschylus, Sophocles, and Euripides, for our wise magistrate Lycurgus has given heed that they shall not disappear from the orchestra and the stage of Dionysus ; but we should also listen with attention to the inspired teachings of the pupils of Plato in the Academy, to the subtle discussions of Aristotle and his school in the Lyceum,

to the eloquent, but diffuse lectures of Zeno in
the ' Painted Porch ' (*Stoa Poikilē*), and from
time to time we should glance into the tempting
' garden ' of the noble sceptic Epicurus.   And
all these elements would enter into our faith—
into what for us forms the essence of the ' religion
of ancient Greece ', as set forth in this book.

The reader must not be surprised that I
address myself not merely to the educated man,
but to the educated believer—it matters not
whether he believes with mind or heart or
memory.   It is exceedingly strange that I am the
first student to formulate a principle which soon,
I hope, will become a truism : ' As a man
bereft of artistic feeling cannot understand
Greek art, so one who lacks religious feeling
cannot understand Greek religion.'   Religious
feeling is a magic wand that trembles every
time we pass by the pure gold of religious faith,
but is not stirred by lead or tinsel.   Whoever
possesses it will easily orient himself in the
labyrinth of legends and ceremonies of ancient
Greece ; whoever does not possess it will find no
aid in erudition.   The imposing work of Otto
Gruppe may serve as an awful example ; it is
unbelievably exhaustive ; it is one of the works
that are indispensable for every investigator
of our field.   But at the same time—it is all
that any one could desire except religion : its
contents could never be an object of faith for
any man.   Being himself an atheist, the author

feels no difference between the living and the
dead in those phenomena which are entitled
' Greek religion '.

To be sure, the other extreme, fanaticism, is
no less barren.   Any one who regards as pagans
and infidels all men of another faith, had best
not touch Greek religion.   Here too art may
serve as an analogy.   Not only the man bereft
of artistic feeling, but also the man who is
exclusively and unreservedly devoted to one of
several hostile tendencies in art, will prove
incapable of appreciating the works of the Greek
chisel.

Thus, reader, we have made a compact.   I
pray you light in your heart the bright torch of
religious feeling and leave at home the dim rushlight of sectarianism : then the majestic temple
of Greek religion will show you its marvels.

II

THE DEIFICATION OF NATURE

For the ancient Greek a consciousness of the mysterious life of the nature that surrounded him was perhaps the deepest foundation of his religious feeling. A consciousness not only of life, but of life infused with spirit ; and not only with spirit, but with divinity. For a man of our own times this is a matter which requires explanation before all others.

The expression ' life ' must be understood in a different sense from that in which we usually contrast ' living ' nature, that is, the organic world of animals and plants, with ' dead ' nature, that is, the inorganic mineral kingdom. For the consciousness of the Greek, dead nature did not exist ; all nature was life, spirit, divinity. It was divine not only in its meadows and forests, in its springs and rivers, but equally divine in the measureless, surging expanse of its seas and in the silent immobility of its mountain wastes. And in these last even more than elsewhere. Here, where our attention is not absorbed by the separate lives of the groves and glades, here

more strongly do we feel the one united life of
the goddess herself, the imperishable source of
all those separate lives, the great mother—
Earth.   She is worshipped amid the white crags,
' goddess of the hills, all-fostering Earth, mother
of Zeus most high ' (Sophocles, *Philoctetes*, 391 :
tr. Jebb).

One of the Russian poets, Lermontov, in his
beautiful lyric, ' When the yellowing meadow
waveth ', has almost succeeded in attaining this
feeling.   Yet he has stopped half way.   I perceive his failure in the last line of the poem :
' And I see God *in the heavens* '.   Here one feels
the poison introduced by Judaism into Christianity, and through it into the souls of the heirs
of Hellenism.   Why ' in the heavens ' ?   Is it
there that ' the yellowing meadow waveth ' ?
Thus in very truth the religion of the Old
Testament violently tears our natural feeling of
gratitude away from that which immediately
calms and caresses us, and diverts it to a hypothetical Creator : ' He who walketh along the
road and " repeateth " [the Law] and stoppeth
his repetition and saith, " How fair is that tree "
—to him the Scripture accounteth that as sin,
depriving him of the right to life ' (*Mishna :
Pirke Aboth*, ch. iii.).

The ancient Greek was more fortunate ; for
him this depressing turning aside from the
straight road was not necessary ; he felt and
saw god in the road itself, in the yellowing

meadow, in the fragrant grove, in the ripening grace of the garden. He surrounded himself and his human life with a whole swarm of deities of nature, now kindly, now threatening, but always sympathetic. And what is most important, he succeeded in establishing a spiritual union with those deities, in looking at their life through the prism of his own consciousness, and in infusing them with a living understanding of himself. To him the Nostradamus of *Faust* would not address these words of reproach :

> The spirit-world no closures fasten ;
> Thy sense is shut, thy heart is dead.
>
> [Tr. TAYLOR.]

After the fall of the ancient world even this gladdening consciousness vanished from the souls of men, yet not without a trace : the ancient Christian religions preserved the germs of it, which in the best representatives of those religions even produced very beautiful fruit, as for example in St. Francis of Assisi, when from beneath the accretions of Judaism there was revealed to him the true, antique foundation of Christianity. . . . But let us return to the Greek.

Out of the earth, from a crevice in the rocks, gushes a cool spring, creating green life around it and quenching the thirst of the flocks and of their shepherd : this is a goddess, a nymph, a naiad. Let us thank her for her good will by good will, let us shelter her current with a roof, let us hollow out a basin beneath her, in order that in its gleaming surface she may contemplate her divine form.   On appointed days let us not forget to cast her a wreath of field flowers, and to redden her bright waters with the blood of a lamb slain in her honour.   On the other hand, if we come to her in time of doubt and anguish of spirit and incline our ears to her murmur, she will remember us and will whisper to us salutary counsel or a word of comfort.   And if the place whence she draws her bright waters is suited to human habitation, a city may arise there, and a whole people will worship her, all Hellas will glorify her.   Such is Callirrhoë in Athens, Dirce in Thebes, Pirene in Corinth.   Each morning the girls of the city will gather at the naiad's sanctuary, in order to fill their jars with her water and to delight her kindly ears with girlish prattle, and in her purifying waters the inhabitants of the city will bathe their new-born children.

A stream flows, unites with another stream, and forms a *river* ; here the concept of good will gives way to another concept—of strength.   To be sure, Greece has no great rivers ; the most important of them cannot be compared even to the Cam of England or the Charles of Massachusetts.   And yet in flood-time even they can cause no little devastation, casting themselves on the cultivated fields and breaking down trees in their way with the violent rush of an enraged bull. Therefore they are represented in the form of bulls or half-bulls. Their wrath, however, is a rare phenomenon, called forth ordinarily by the sins of the inhabitants, who have passed false judgment in the market-place and driven forth Justice from their assemblies; at other times they are beneficent deities, fructifying with their moisture not only the neighbouring meadows and forests, but, thanks to irrigation ditches, the whole plain; in Greece with its scanty rainfall they are veritable ' nourishers ' of their land. In return they also enjoy worship. At appropriate places men build temples to them and make offerings; they invoke them in public prayers, and absolutely all boys, when they reach the age of ephebi (that is, puberty), consecrate to them the first lock of their hair that is cut off. Such are the river Cephissus for Athens, Ismenus for Thebes, Inachus for Argos. Being the nourishers of the whole land, they have also a mysterious influence on the human harvest— childless parents turn to them with a prayer for offspring. And if among the multitude of Greek proper names we find such as Cephisodotus, Ismenias, or Anaximander (that is, probably, -meander) it is a superfluous question to ask where those who bear them were born. But a river-god was not merely the nourisher of the inhabitants of his country in times of peace; in times of war he was their support, and not only in a physical but in a religious sense. The

Erasinus is a very tiny little river, a mere streamlet, and yet the Spartan general Cleomenes on his expedition to Argos did not venture to pass over it, as the river-god, after many sacrifices, did not give him permission to do so.

The *grove* also is alive in its deity—and not only as a whole, but in the person of the separate trees. Here too we have nymphs, nymphs of the trees, *dryads*. There are many of them— and hence comes their happiness : on moon-light nights they come forth from the trees and join in choral dance, led by their queen, Artemis, goddess of the groves. Yet even a solitary tree is divine, if it be strong and beautiful—like that plane tree on the bank of the Ilissus in Athens, under which Socrates and Phaedrus once rested.

There is the lofty and spreading plane tree, and the agnus castus high and clustering, in the fullest blossom and the greatest fragrance ; and the stream which flows beneath the plane tree is deliciously cold to the feet. Judging from the ornaments and images, this must be a spot sacred to Acheloüs and the nymphs.
[PLATO, *Phaedrus*, 230 B : tr. JOWETT.]

For good will one must pay with good will, as we have already seen : and is not this a proof of good will—the cool shade in the heat of the day, the quiet murmur of the rustling leaves, the song, if not always of birds, of the grasshoppers dear to the Grecian heart ? In all this one feels love ; and where love is, there is God likewise.

But the nymphs know another love as well.

For the grove and the forest are an eternal, incessant fructifying and creating of the physical life by which nature lives. For the Greek his nymph is unceasing fertility, an unceasing love-play with the wanton representatives of the fructifying element of the forest, the *satyrs*—and sometimes also with that god who at home in Arcadia was the supreme god of creation and fructifying, but who became for the rest of Greece the wanderer god, the kindly and careless Hermes. All this does not concern mortals—and yet there are exceptions. It sometimes happens that even a mortal, thanks to his beauty, becomes worthy of the caresses of a divine nymph ; such is the story, for example, of a certain beautiful shepherd, Daphnis. The love of the goddess brought him no good fortune ; he ventured to betray her for a mortal woman, and therefore, blind man, he was punished with physical blindness. And whenever in a grove, in a clearing, there was found an infant of marvellous beauty and strength, foolish folk vexed themselves with guesses and gossip, but experienced old women knew that it was the child of a nymph.

And aloft, ever higher—on Hymettus and Pentelicon—here forests and trees no longer occur, here only goats go from time to time to nibble the prickly herbage that peeps forth from between white blocks of limestone. Here more and more frequently one may see naked

masses of rock, full of fantastic pinnacles and
grottos.   This is the kingdom of the *oreads*,
nymphs who dwell in the mountain wastes.
Here in the grottos they weave thin, invisible
fabrics, sweetening their labours with song ; no
mortal ever ventures to hearken to them or to
watch them, but their looms may be seen by day,
if one enter the grotto—of course after repeating
an appropriate prayer.   They are pleased also
with other tokens of reverence—if one anoint
with oil the rocky pinnacle or hang on it a girdle,
or make a modest offering on the altar at the
entrance to the grotto.   And they will pay their
debt : who but they guards the precious spring
that gushes forth at the summit ?   Who but
they saves our she-goat from going astray amid
the crags ?

But no : here they have a rival.   He is a guest
from Arcadia, of comparatively recent adoption
into the assembly of the gods of Greece as a
whole, the fantastic guardian spirit of goats,
Pan the goat-legged.   If we call him a ' god ', it
is simply because we designate by that name any
powerful, immortal being of whatever sort ; in
reality we understand perfectly the difference
between him and the great gods of Olympus.
Later the evil conscience of a religion which has
cut loose from nature and Mother Earth will
change him into the devil ; but we love him and
respect him as the kindly god of the mountains
with the melodious pipes.   To be sure, we know

of many of his strange pranks, not to speak of those of which his neighbours the oreads might tell us. At noonday he takes a nap (that is ' the hour of Pan'), and woe to the incautious shepherd who ventures at that time to amuse himself by playing his pipes! When the awakened Pan thrusts forth his shaggy brow from behind a crag, when he shouts over all the countryside, then the frightened goats will rush downward over the stones, overturning in their path both one another and the terror-stricken shepherd. Never will he forget Pan and his ' panic ' fear !

The earth is divine, but the *sea* is equally so. For the Greeks it has a deeper significance than for any other nation, even among those situated on the sea ; for it not only encircles their shores, but lovingly penetrates their land with innumerable bays and straits, refreshing it and furnishing on every hand convenient water communication. And so the Greeks become fused with it ; every one of them is a born sailor and mariner. And therefore great is their honour for the god Posidon and his spouse Amphitrite, who dwells deep beneath the blue surface and rules over a multitude of fishes, crabs, and other strange and monstrous denizens of her moist kingdom. Posidon, however, is not only the god of an element, but a revered member of the Olympian family, and we shall speak further of him.

Immediately connected with the sea are the sea-nymphs, or *nereids*, ' the personification of the gentle waves of the sea ', as some men will later speak of them in a dry and stupid fashion. Clearly those men will never attain the grace of beholding the nereids themselves, in their proper form, silver-footed, as they sport about on a serene day, racing with the dolphins, their golden hair flashing over the crests of the waves. Great is that grace, and yet it is nothing in comparison to that which they bestow on their elect, as did Thetis, who made Peleus happy in her love, and, a goddess, bore to him the most beautiful and the most noble hero in the world, Achilles. Of this a common mortal may not dream ; he prays to the potent goddesses for a successful voyage, and will not forget to show them due gratitude in the form of a votive gift and a sacrifice.

The nereids are the nymphs of the sea, but they too have their satyrs. These are the *tritons*, youths with tails like those of fishes. With them it is better not to make acquaintance ; they are, as those same wiseacres will say, ' the personification of the stormy waves ' Behold, the clouds have obscured the blue of the sky, the sea has grown ominously black and ruffled— and suddenly in the distance is heard a loud, prolonged roar. . . . It is the tritons blowing on their conch shells ; it is the prelude to the coming storm. Then, sailors, furl your sails, labour with your oars—and at the same time

pray ardently to Posidon, to the nereids, and
to your protectors on the sea, the twin Dioscuri,
Castor and Polydeuces.   Your prayers will be
heard, two feeble flames will gleam at opposite
ends of the yard—it is they in person, the divine
Dioscuri—they give you an omen of salvation.

The sea also has its Pan ; he is *Proteus*, the
shepherd of a flock of strange beasts of the sea,
and himself a very strange creature.   As to his
form it is difficult to say anything : he changes
it continually, like the sea itself, but he is most
frequently simply an old man of the sea.   His
whimsies are well known to his daughter Idothea,
a daughter who shows small respect for her
father, but who is gracious to sailors.   Like her
is Leucothea, now also a goddess of the sea, but
once the wronged wife Ino. . . .   Here and there
in Greece Bacchic mysteries are celebrated in
her honour, but in Attica she is known mostly
from Homer, as the kind deliverer of Odysseus.

And further—whoever has felt the irresistible
charm of the sea on a serene day, when the sun-
beams play on its surface and the waves lap
gently, and it is impossible to restrain one's
longing to plunge into that blue expanse—he
knows also the sea-god Glaucus (or ' the blue ').
And there is yet another, fatal yearning—when
after your long struggle the waves have overwhelmed you, when your arms droop, and in
your ears rings a melancholy and tempting sum-
mons to soothing death.   That is the *sirens*

singing on a distant, desolate crag, amid the roaring billows : God grant that none may hear their song !

Finally, the third element, the *heavens*. It is called Uranus, but that name awakens in us no religious feeling. Theologians say that once the primordial Mother Earth produced from herself Uranus and that he became the element that fructified her and caused her to bear the Titans and the Titanids ; and they add that finally her own posterity began to weigh upon her and that at her request the youngest of the Titans, Cronus, deprived his father of regenerative power—such was the first sin among the denizens of the heavens. These guesses do not bind us ; the undoubted lord of the heavens is *Zeus*, the son of Cronus (' the fulfiller '). His character is not in the least degree derived from his significance as a god of nature, but for the moment we are speaking only of Zeus ' the cloud-gatherer ', who gathers the storm in the murky sky, of Zeus ' the caster of thunderbolts ', who throws his fiery bolt at the high places of earth, against lofty trees and buildings, at all that is too lofty, as a lesson to mortals. Him above all we must try to appease by prayer and sacrifice. . . . By sacrifice ! But how ? The heavens are not the earth and not the sea ; a hand bearing gifts can never reach them. Verily we should be eternally separated from the king of the ether, had not the friend of mankind, the Titan *Prometheus*, brought us secretly the heavenly *fire*. The fire aspires to return to its heavenly habitation, it rises to it in the form of flying smoke—then let it carry with it also the smoke and steam of our sacrifice. A fiery sacrifice is the true tribute to the gods of the heavens.

The denizens of the divine heavens are likewise divine; and above all, of course, its great stars, *Helios*, the Sun, and *Selene*, the Moon. As to the nature of Helios there are no universally accepted ideas. Many men still think that he is a divine youth, who traverses in a golden chariot the 'firmament' of heaven, and that the blinding light which we see is really the gleam of his chariot. For us it is a riddle how, vanishing in the west, he rises in the east : of old, men thought that by night he made his return voyage to the east by a river called Oceanus, which encircles the earth, but to-day it is a matter fairly well proved that Helios and the other stars sink beneath the horizon and during our night shine in the lands of the blessed on the surface of the earth opposite our own. Once Anaxagoras taught us that Helios was a gigantic glowing ball, as large as the Peloponnesus. Many men then thought that he exaggerated— just think of it, as the whole Peloponnesus !— and others called him an atheist, because he changed a god into a ball, and a glowing one at

that. We will leave to the astronomers of
Alexandria all scientific investigations into the
forms and motions of the heavenly bodies ; a
god remains a god without regard to the garment
which it pleases him to wear. And for us Helios
is above all a purifying god ; as his blazing
beams by the force of their heat make harmless
all putrefaction, so his spirit annihilates all stain,
every nightmare of anxious slumber. When he
rises we hail him with a greeting and a prayer,
and we relate to him our disquieting dreams, that
he may purify our souls from them.

Selene we worship and love because she illumines our nights with her kindly light ; by her
we reckon the days of our lives, always beginning
each month at the new moon and ending it at
the new moon. Therefore the month is divided
into the time of the waxing moon, that of the
full moon, and that of the waning moon, approxi-
mately ten days apiece. Besides this lovers may
entrust Selene with their joyous or their melancholy secrets : the good goddess will not deny
them counsel. As to her further powers, one may
question the enchantresses, above all those of
Thessaly, who by their songs can bring her down
from her heavenly paths and force her to serve
their charms : that is a domain of sinful practices,
justly persecuted in well-ordered states.

The heaven by night is full of marvels. . . .
There is ' the evening star ', *Hesperus*, fairest of
stars, ' sharer of the throne of Aphrodite '—why

so, lovers know well. There is the group of
seven stars, the *Pleiades* ; they are as it were the
nymphs of heaven. As ' doves ' (*peleiades*) they
bring to Zeus ambrosia ; yet at the same time
they are comely goddesses, daughters of the
Titan Atlas, and spouses of the gods, as was that
Maia who on the summit of Cyllene bore Hermes
to Zeus. There is the (Great) *Bear* : such was
the form which Zeus gave to his chosen one, the
nymph Callisto, whom previously the jealous
Hera had changed into a wild beast of the same
name. The queen of heaven was not pleased
at the honour bestowed upon her rival, and
therefore she prevailed upon Oceanus, the god
of the river which encircles the earth, not to
permit her to enjoy a refreshing bath in his
bright waters. There is *Arcturus* or *Boötes* : he
was placed there to guard the Bear (*Arcturus*,
' the guard of the bear ' ; *Boötes*, ' the cowherd ').
There is *Orion*, the passionate ' lover ', who dared
to raise his hand against Artemis. Many, very
many such tales are in circulation about the
meaning of the mysterious figures in which the
stars of the sky are arranged ; but all this is
' poetical religion ', rather a play of the imagination than a matter of faith. The only exception
is the ' Heavenly Twins ', the Dioscuri, Castor
and Polydeuces. When after a storm at sea the
clouds are parted, and on a patch of night sky
shines forth the kindly light of these twin stars,
then the sailor in ardent gratitude raises towards

them his palms : the appearance of those deities who have always protected him is bringing him salvation.

When we speak of heavenly phenomena, we must not omit the *winds :* they too are divine. They are distinguished by the direction from which they blow and are appropriately characterized. The wind ' from beyond the mountains ', Boreas, brings cold, but it disperses the clouds ; in Attica it enjoyed special honour, since it blew from Thrace, a country on which the Athenian state had special views, of a political nature. Its opponent, Notus, blows from the parched deserts of Africa, and, flying over the sea, gathers up its moisture, which it later allows to fall in the form of rain. The west wind, Zephyrus, in Greece was not necessarily regarded as a spring wind, as it was by the Romans ; it is rather a strong, violent wind, like its opponent, Eurus.

If the reader has grown weary of contemplating the separate parts of this divine nature, let him now gather together his impressions, let him concentrate his feeling of worship and adoration on the two great, dominating elements, *Father Zeus* and *Mother Earth.* In them is inherent the primary, fundamental dualism of Greek religion. One is the fructifying force, the other the fructified ; their mutual attraction is that primordial, holy *love*, that Eros which has created all the life of the living world, and which is also the type and the justification of human love.

Lovingly the Heaven yearns to fructify the Earth.

[Compare AESCHYLUS, frag. 44.]

Thus does Aphrodite defend the human love of Hypermnestra and Lynceus, for the sake of which Hypermnestra has violated the stern command of her father. Thus the heaven fructifies the earth with its warmth, its light, its rain ; it is the eternally male and the earth is the eternally female element. The Greek language expresses this religion with absolute clearness : in it *ouranos* is of masculine gender, *gaia* of feminine. Latin, in which *coelum* is of neuter gender, and Slavic, in which *nebo* is also of neuter gender, are far less clear ; but on the other hand the words for *earth* in all the Indo-European languages are of feminine gender. And if anything can prove how inaccessible to our own feeling is the Egyptian religion, it is the fact that in it the earth is a god, and the sky a goddess.

Yet why does Aeschylus term the Heavens (Uranus) and not Zeus, the universal fructifier? He might with equal confidence have mentioned the latter ; Indian, Latin, and Germanic analogies prove that the original meaning of the name *Zeus* was ' heavens ' or ' sky '. Once on a time the dualism of Zeus and Earth had been of great importance in Greek religion ; the oldest and most beautiful myths are founded on it, and furthermore the famous confession of faith of the Sibyl of Dodona recognizes it :

> Zeus was, Zeus is, and Zeus shall be.   O mighty Zeus !
> Earth yieldeth fruits ; therefore ye name her Mother Earth.   [Tr. LINFORTH.]

But as in a man's immediate feeling the mother who bore him and nourished him is physically nearer than the mediate causer of his birth, the father, so of the two cosmic parents of all life the father at an earlier date took on a spiritual nature, while only Mother Earth re-mained in immediate proximity to human consciousness.

She is the oldest of the assembly of the Olym-pian gods : Greece built many temples to her, under the simple name of Mother (*Mētēr*)—as in Athens and Olympia—long before there was introduced from Asia Minor the cult of a kindred but barbaric goddess, the Great Mother of the gods, or Cybele. She was represented as a stately woman, of maternal form, with only the upper half of her body emerging from her native element.

The Greek cherished truly filial feelings for this parent and nourisher—both love and wor-ship—to a degree absolutely incomprehensible to the denatured consciousness of our contempora-ries. To be sure, we too are capable of going to war for our fatherland ; but what is this ' physi-cal patriotism ' in comparison with that which

filled the Greek with ardour at the thought of his
Mother Earth, with that which found expression
in the marvellous verses of Aeschylus :

> You meanwhile
> It now behoves—both him who faileth yet
> Of youth's fair prime, and him whose bloom is past,
> His body's vigour nursing to the full,
> And each with vigour that befits him best—
> The State to aid and shrines of native gods,
> That ne'er their honours be erased ; to aid
> Your children too, and this your Mother Earth,
> Beloved nurse, who, while your childish limbs
> Crept on her friendly plain, all nurture-toil
> Full kindly entertained, and fostered you
> Her denizens to be, in strait like this
> Shield-bearing champions, trusty in her cause.
>
> [AESCHYLUS, *The Seven against Thebes*, 10-20 :
> tr. SWANWICK.]

Agricultural reforms are now the question of
the day, and the motto ' the land for the people '
is regarded as the last word in democracy. To
the Greek it would have seemed blasphemy : no,
not the land for the people, but the people for
the land ! The needs of the land should be in
the foreground. It is of them that Solon thought,
when he carried through the first agricultural
reform known to history; it was her favour that
he wished to gain for himself :

> Turning now to my own case, and considering first
> the objects for which I brought the people together,
> you ask me why I stopped before I had achieved those
> objects. The answer to this question may be found

in the corroborative evidence which will be given
before the tribunal of Time by the black Earth, the
supreme mother of the divinities of Olympus. I
removed the stones of her bondage which had been
planted everywhere, and she who was a slave before
is now free.

> [Quoted by ARISTOTLE, *Constitution of Athens*, 12 :
> tr. LINFORTH.]

This is true, far-seeing democracy. The earth
is more than the people, for it is the source of
the life of all the descendants of people now
living. To the Greek this profoundly true and
beneficent dogma was disclosed by his immediate
religious feeling.

In view of this can we marvel at the pride felt
by the Athenians at the thought that they were
' autochthones ', that is, that their forefathers
were in a literal sense born from the land which
they themselves still inhabited ? We find this
thought in every encomium on Athens, whether
in verse or in prose, so that we see clearly how
precious it was to the inhabitants of the city of
Pallas. And it is no accident that from Athens
came the thinker who dressed this thought in
the form of a philosophic doctrine—extending
it, to be sure, to all humanity—Epicurus.
Mother Earth, he maintains, has now ceased to
give birth ; she no longer brings into the world
either men or other living creatures, except for
some low species—and we men of to-day may be
indulgent to this result of diligent but inadequate
observation. But in the time of her fruitful

youth, Epicurus continues, it was otherwise ; then she brought forth the first men immediately from her womb.   And immediately after this act there occurred within her the same phenomenon as in the body of a woman who has given birth :   an excess of fluids was transformed into milk, and all over her surface elevations grew up from which gushed forth vivifying streams for the new-born children.

[*De Rerum Natura*, v, 821, 822.]

Quare etiam atque etiam *maternum* nomen adepta
Terra tenet merito—

Wherefore, again and again I say, the earth with good title has gotten and keeps the name of *mother* (since she of herself gave birth to mankind).

[Tr. Munro.]

Such is the conclusion of the ardent disciple of Epicurus, Lucretius.

And one can also understand that under the watchful care of this mother, and surrounded by her devoted children, the Greek never felt himself alone; he never knew that feeling of desertion which a man in our day so often experiences as a just punishment for his ingratitude and impiety.   I will cite one example of many.   I will remind you of the fate of Philoctetes. Deserted by his comrades on the desolate island of Lemnos, lame and with the eternal pain of a wound on his leg that refused to heal, it would seem that no man could be more unfortunate. Despite this, I beg you to observe in what manner, after ten years' torture in this wilderness, he bids it farewell—yet the reader, trained in modern aesthetics, must not seek to show his own cleverness ; he must not seek for poetic adorn- ments and licences, but must take every word simply, in its literal meaning.

> Yet ere I part I fain would bid farewell.
> Home of my vigils, rocky cell,
> Nymphs of the streams and grass-fringed shore,
> Caves where the deep-voic'd breakers' roar,
> When through the cavern's open mouth,
> Borne on the wings of the wild South,
> E'en to my dwelling's inmost lair,
> The rain and spray oft drench'd my hair ;
> And oft responsive to my groan
> Mount Hermaeum made his moan ;
> O Lycian fount, O limpid well,
> I thought with you all time to dwell ;
> And now I take my last farewell.
> Sea-girt Lemnos, hear my prayer !
> Bid thy guest a voyage fair,
> Speed him to the land where he,
> Borne by mighty Destiny,
> And the god at whose decree
> All was ordered, fain would be.
>   [SOPHOCLES, *Philoctetes*, 1452-68 : tr. STORR.]

But this feeling of orphanhood was only one punishment of the Mother for her recreant sons ; another punishment was still more terrible.

Ancient Israel was the direct opposite of Hellas. Led by its God, the Lord of Hosts, it entered into ' the promised land ' as a stranger and a con- queror. It cherished no filial feelings for that

land, which had never been its mother, but had
been populated by evil spirits.   And it grafted
its own predatory, mandatory relation to the
land upon those religions which in some degree
arose from it, upon Christianity and Islam.
The earth was transformed from a mother into
a slave, obedient, but vengeful.   To be sure,
Christianity has never ventured to become the
scourge of the earth—its other foundation, that
of Greek and Roman life, was too powerful
within it.   But truly terrible was the devastation which Islam brought with it.   I pray you,
look into ancient sources and convince yourself
what flourishing lands during the epoch of
Greco-Roman culture were Asia Minor, ' the
land of five hundred cities ', Syria, and northern
Africa—and then call to mind what they are
to-day.   Verily, the God of Mohammed has
devastated with fire that gigantic tract of land ;
the gods of the ancient world had watched over
it with affectionate care.

III

THE CONSECRATION OF WORK

Some one once ventured to assert that the ancient Greeks despised and scorned physical work, and ever since that time this absurd statement has been wandering unchecked through the pages of manuals and compendiums that derive their material at second hand or at tenth hand. Of course, this allegation must have had some basis. It was founded on the opinion of the aristocratic writer Plato and of a few others concerning the injurious effect on man's mental processes of artisan labour, which chains him to the workshop and at the same time directs his thoughts exclusively towards gain. But, to say nothing of the fact that Plato and his fellow-writers are not speaking of all physical labour, and in particular not of labour in the fields, what warrant have we to make Plato's words representative of the view of Greece as a whole? Why not oppose to them the Homeric Odysseus, who appeals with equal pride to his endurance at the time of harvest and to his deeds in war?— Odysseus, who with his own hands made himself

his marriage bed and the boat that saved him !
Why should we not mention Hesiod, who
dedicated to his heedless brother Perses his
Works and Days, with their guiding thought,
' To work, foolish Perses ', and with the famous
verse :

Now work is no disgrace, sloth is disgrace (verse 311).

Mother Earth, who bestowed upon her beloved
Hellas so many precious gifts, did not bless her
with fertility of soil : the Greek people had to
gain their scanty sustenance by labour, of which
the inhabitants of kindly plains can have no
conception. Stone terraces had to be built on
the slopes of the mountains, in order to prevent
the winter rains from washing away a fertile
layer which no one who has ever visited those
regions will call ' black loam ' ; reservoirs had
to be dug in the stony ground at appropriate
places, in order to preserve the precious rain
water for the rainless months ; rivers had to be
diverted into irrigation ditches in order to
secure for the fields their needful portion of
moisture—the Cephissus of Athens did not even
reach the sea, being entirely absorbed by ditches.
And all this was only the beginning of the work
that the Greeks had to undertake !

As we see from this—but, of course, not from
this alone—the labour of man rather seriously
disturbed the calm of the divine life of the
Mother and of the children whom she bore :
how then do they react to this intrusion ? A

compact was needed, which should define the
rights and the duties of man; a divine service
was needed, in exchange for the service which the
divinity had agreed to render to man : in other
words, a need was felt for the *consecration of
work by religion.* This was secured, and moreover, to a greater degree than by any other
nation. If the abundant phenomena, partially
set forth in the preceding chapter, permit us to
regard ancient religion as a religion of nature,
so those to which we are now passing will give
us a perfect right to see in it a religion of work.
But, as I must emphasize at the outset, not
merely of work, but—*of the joy of work.*

Man in the hunting stage of social development disturbed least the normal course of the
life of nature ; for at bottom man the hunter
differs but little from the lion, the wolf, the vul-
ture, and other predatory creatures whose life
forms a single whole with the life of the rest of
nature. He differs but little, and yet he differs :
through reason, through an ingenuity which
rises above nature, and which has led him to
invent nets, arrows, and spears, to tame dogs,
and to devise a whole hunting equipment that
threatens with extinction the living creatures
of the forests and mountains.

So man must receive the laws that guide his
activity from the goddess whom he serves as a
hunter—from *Artemis.* She is the mighty
guardian of all manner of beasts and birds ;

equally dear to her heart are the young of all living creatures, even though they be the young of beasts and birds of prey. She permits man to make free use of adult individuals, but she does not permit him to destroy the species—and an Erinys punishes him if disobedient. Thus the nests of birds are sacred, and pregnant females are sacred ; if one of them falls into the hands of a hunter, his duty is ' to let it go free for Artemis '.

This humane relation to animals, which so favourably distinguished the ancient Greeks from their descendants of to-day, and which found expression for example in the beautiful saying, ' Even dogs have their Erinyes ', was to a notable degree called forth by the fact that the Greeks felt upon them the gaze of Artemis, who heard the cries of tortured crea-tures and condemned the offender to punish-ment at the hands of the dread goddesses of the underworld, the guardians of the great co pact by which the world lives. And in t epoch of agricultural life this right of beasts kind treatment was confirmed anew in the m holy of Greek mysteries, those of Eleusis : o of the commandments of Triptolemus ran, ' I no wrong to beasts '.

As we see, these beneficent precepts, which modern states have been developed by tl civil law in comparatively recent times (and which are observed with a conscientiousness with

which we are all familiar!) were enjoined on the
Greek by his religion, as the immediate consequence of his filial relation to Mother Earth.

And it is self-evident that for the happy issue
of a hunt a man also owed gratitude to Artemis.
In general, whoever would gain a due conception
of the pure beauty of the relations of a hunter
to this goddess, who was his guardian, should
make the acquaintance of the young hunter
Hippolytus in Euripides' tragedy of that name.
Yet man must not think that when he has
emerged from the hunting stage of social development into another he may forget the virgin
goddess of the forests. Thus sinned Oeneus of
Calydon : gathering an abundant harvest from
the fields, he honoured with the first fruits the
other gods, but he neglected Artemis. The
goddess reminded him of her existence by send-
ing against his growing crops a monstrous boar
and thereby calling forth the tragedy of the
'Calydonian hunt', in which she played the same
part as Aphrodite in the tragedy of the Trojan
War.

And yet the shedding of blood in hunting,
even though sanctified by law, troubled the
sensitive conscience of the Greek. He felt the
need of subjecting himself on his return home to
a religious purification ; and not he himself alone
must be purified but even his hunting dogs :

For Zeus himself ordained this law for men :
The forest beasts, and fish, and winged birds

May without sin on one another feed,
For to them Justice is unknown ; to man
However he gave Justice.

[HESIOD, *Works and Days*, 276-279.]

On passing from the hunting stage of society
to the *pastoral*, man felt the need of similarly
consecrating to the gods this branch of his work,
of giving to it also the forms of divine service.
Obviously he must pay his first debt of gratitude to that god who had permitted humanity,
guided by himself, to attain that higher stage of
culture. This was *Hermes*, the god of Arcadia,
of a land which, remaining predominantly
pastoral even in historic times, preserved better
than other regions the traditions of the pastoral
epoch. He it was who brought down from
Olympus the first herd of cows and gave them to
mortals : this gift had at first a deep meaning,
similar to that of the rape of fire by Prometheus, and only the ill repute into which the
Arcadians fell in historic times, as vagabonds
and thieves, permitted singers to transform even
this beneficent act of their god into a clever
thievish trick—for 'many things do bards devise'
in which even they themselves do not believe. In
some other places shepherds worshipped *Apollo :*
once on a time he himself, in order to expiate
the slaying of the Python (or the Cyclops) had
deigned for a whole year to be the shepherd of
Admetus, King of Thessaly—both the flocks
and their owner prospered well with such a shep-

herd. With *Pan* we are already acquainted; he
too came from Arcadia, where he was regarded
as the son of Hermes. And the inevitable
assistants of all these gods were ' the nymphs of
the waters and the meadows ', who afforded
moisture to the pastures in the burning days
of summer; to them also the shepherds built
unpretentious shrines, and they worshipped
them with prayers, gifts, and sacrifices.

They also worshipped them—and along with
them other pastoral gods—with the music of
the lyre or the pipes, and with songs. The lyre
was invented by Hermes, who once happened
to find the dry shell of a tortoise, a splendid
sounding-board for strings, as he at once observed.
He used his lyre to pay for the herd of Apollo,
which he had stolen, and thereafter Apollo
employed it along with the cithara, which after
all was only a perfected lyre. The pipes—in
Greek *syrinx*—were, as we already know, the
instrument of Pan. The pastoral life with its
abundant leisure furnished opportunity for playing on musical instruments; this playing gave
joy to the soul of the player and at the same time
was useful to the flocks, which, while listening
to the familiar sounds, were in no danger of
straying away. From it there developed a
special branch of work—that is to say, of intellectual work—and therefore we shall speak of
it later.

The care of herds and its kindred occupation, bee-keeping, gave man a natural, bloodless nourishment—both for himself and for his gods : milk, honey, and, in the third place, water—such was the composition of the oldest ' nephalian ' (that is, sober, without wine) liquid sacrifice. But man could not remain long in ignorance that goats, sheep, and, above all, cows could also feed him with their nutritious and delicious meat. Not without trembling did he profit by this discovery ; in order to do so he was forced to slay his fosterer, to shed her blood.   An echo of this terror was still preserved in historic times in the ceremonies of the festival termed the *Bouphonia* (that is, ' the bull-slaying ', evidently ' murder ' and not ' slaughter '). The bull was led to the altar of Zeus, on which lay an offering of plants dedicated to the god.   When the foolish beast began to feed, the attendant priest slew it with a blow of an axe and straightway took to flight ; in his absence judgment was passed on the axe ; special parts of the bull were used for a sacrifice to Zeus, while men consumed the remainder.   In historical times men of education laughed not a little at this savage rite and its naïve craft ; but it will be more just on our part to appreciate the delicacy of feeling which here found expression in the idea beneath the rite, that one cannot without sin shed the blood of a domesticated animal.

Finally comes the ordered state of social

development, that of *agriculture*. This brings
with it the existence of property, which requires
defence ; it gives rise to a fixed abode and a state
order ; man's work receives its highest consecration in the service of the god by the entire
state. A cycle of public festivals was established in Athens and other Greek cities, on the
basis of a compact with Delphi, in whose hands
rested the supreme guidance of Hellas in religious
matters : hence the dominating part played in
these festivals by Apollo and Artemis, in whose
honour most of the months were named. Yet
at the same time these festivals are the *apotheosis
of work*, and in so lofty, so solemn, so beautiful a
form as no other nation of the world has ever
known. I am forced to limit myself to a brief
characterization of them, and therefore shall not
depart from the confines of Athens.

The goddess of field work is Demeter, really
one of the variants of Mother Earth, as we may
judge with certainty from her name (*Dē-mētēr*—
' soil-mother '). For the Greek she was the
symbol of the ripening grain, in the waves of
which we may perceive her even to-day. And
therefore this ' mother ' has a ' daughter ', Cora,
the symbol of the kernels from which the grain
for the next year will spring forth. How from
this mystery of the reviving grain Hellenic
wisdom deduced the further mystery of the
immortality of the soul we shall discuss later; on
this amazing synthesis rests the most holy of the

solemnities of Demeter, the Eleusinian festival
and its mysteries ; but originally this was only
the festival of tillage (*proërosia*). Solemn likewise was the day on which the stay of Cora with
her lord in the underworld was half concluded,
but still more solemn was the festival of the
harvest itself. And here the thought of the
Greek, of the Athenian, did not remain fixed on
the mere physical significance of the action :
the giver of crops appeared to him as the found-
ress of all settled life, which is characterized by
the stability of the marriage bond and by family
life ; he beheld in her his ' lawgiver ' (*thesmophoros*), and transformed the original harvest
festival into a deeply pondered festival of
family life in general, the *Thesmophoria*, which
was celebrated exclusively by married women.
Schiller has most beautifully depicted the significance of these rites in his *Festival of Eleusis*,
but under an incorrect title ; he has in mind
Demeter Thesmophoros, not the Demeter of
Eleusis.

After field work comes the work of the cultivation of the vine, which was immensely
important in southern lands, and which was
consecrated to *Dionysus*. The development of
Dionysus in Greece was quite the reverse of that
of Demeter. She was transformed from the
modest goddess of the ripening cornfields into a
lawgiver goddess and a goddess of the mysteries
of the world beyond the grave. He made his

appearance in Greece as the god of creative
ecstasy, who also brought to his initiates tidings
of the immortality of the soul ; yet in the public
cult his festival also had to be adapted to human
labour : therefore he was entrusted with the
cultivation of the vine, akin to the ecstasy that
he bestowed, but originally independent of him.
At present we will confine ourselves to this side
of his nature.

The anxiety that Dionysus might bless the
growing, flowering, and fruit-giving vine pertained only to the private cult of the deity ; the
state cared for the vine only after the grapes
were gathered. The cycle of the festivals of
Dionysus opened with the gay *Oschophoria*, or
' bearing of the grapes '. They were borne by
ephebi, chosen youths of the ten phylae (tribes),
from the temple of Dionysus in Athens to the
temple of Pallas in Phalerum ; the clusters of
grapes were the gift of Dionysus to the goddess-
guardian of the land. The other festivals were
connected with various stages of the fermenta-
tion of the young wine: they were the Rural
Dionysia in December, the Lenaea in January,
and the Anthesteria in February. All were
accompanied by ceremonies, partly gay and
partly serious, and were coloured by a multitude of marvellous myths and legends ; but
the most beautiful of all the Dionysiac festivals
was the Great Dionysia in March, established
by Pisistratus. Its founder appreciated the

original significance of the god to whom worship was paid ; for him Dionysus was the god of creative ecstasy : wine became subordinate ; song dominated, and within its sphere the song of songs, tragedy. Whoever prizes the culture of the human race must bow his head reverently before the Great Dionysia ; that festival furnished the occasion for the rise of those mighty creations of human genius, the works of Aeschylus, Sophocles, and Euripides.

Of the remaining branches of field labour, the *culture of trees* in general was also consecrated to Dionysus as ' dendrites ', the god of the gathering forces of spring ; but the Athenian consecrated his olive to his goddess-guardian, Pallas Athena. For it was she who had presented her people with it on that memorable day when the fate of the city was decided. Posidon, wishing to show the people his strength, with a stroke of his trident drew forth a spring of sea water from the rock of the Acropolis ; but Pallas showed men that goodness rather than strength is the highest manifestation of divinity : at her nod there grew forth on that same rock her immortal olive, the venerable progenitor of the time-honoured olive trees in the valley of the Cephissus. They too are venerable : they are called ' moriae ', or ' trees of fate ', for fate punishes any person who touches such a tree with a sacrilegious hand :

Youth shall not mar it by the ravage of his hand, nor any who dwells with old age ; for the

sleepless eye of the Morian Zeus beholds it, and the
gray-eyed Athena.

[SOPHOCLES, *Oedipus at Colonus*, 702-706 :
tr. JEBB.]

The Spartans respected this prohibition during
the Peloponnesian War ; as pious men, they did
not touch the sacred moriae of Pallas.   In those
times men still understood the meaning of piety.
Apart from this matter, however, in Athens the
cult of Pallas as the goddess-guardian of the entire
state naturally obscured her cult as the guardian
of the olive tree : at her magnificent festival, the
Panathenaea, the oil of the olive merely served
as a reward for the victors in the games, to whom
the state presented it in beautiful clay amphorae,
likewise of Athenian workmanship, with symbolic decorations and with the inscription, ' I
come from the Athenian games '—as an eternal
memorial and one worthy of envy.

To Pallas was likewise consecrated the *work of
the artisan* in all its many branches—for she had
the title of *Athena Ergane*, and as such she had
her own holy place on the Acropolis, in front
of the Parthenon, and her yearly festival in
October, at the new moon.   But of all the crafts
one was peculiarly near to her, as a goddess :
this was the art of weaving, the most distinguished of all branches of women's work from
the point of view of artistic perfection.   So at
the annual festival of the Panathenaea there was
deposited on the Acropolis, as a gift to Pallas,

a peplos woven by the most skilled women in Athens, and the bearing of it to her shrine formed the central point of all the solemnities.

Of the other crafts Pallas had under her personal protection that of the potter, the pride of all Attica :

Hear thou our prayer, O Athena, protect thou our kiln
    with thy right hand !
Grant thou success to our pitchers, our pots, and our
    dishes of clay ;
Grant that they prosper in baking and bring us in plenty
    of money !—

thus runs a potter's prayer to her which chance has preserved to us.   As protectress of this craft, she could easily hold in check the malicious little demons of whose destructive acts we learn from the curse that follows the prayer :

Forward now, Fragments and Cracker ; be watchful,
    thou demon, Unquenchable !
Hey now, Smashpot and Bully, now may you wreck this
    man's workshop ;
Ruin the hearth and the house, and overturn all bottom
    upward,
Breaking the kiln and its contents, mid wailing and
    groans from the potter !
                  [Homeric Epigram 14.]

Little demons of like sort presumably infested other crafts as well, but by chance we know nothing of them.

In the work of the smith, however, Pallas had a companion : that man was regarded as a

skilful smith who had been taught his craft by
'*Hephaestus* and Pallas Athena'.   Hephaestus,
as the god of fire ('the volcanic'), was here indispensable.   Athens regarded him with special
respect ; it built him a beautiful temple—
probably that which is still preserved and is
usually called the ' Theseum '—and worshipped
him along with Pallas at a yearly festival (the
' Hephaesteia ' and ' Chalceia ', or ' festival of
the smiths ') at the end of October, before the
coming on of winter, when a reminder of the
beneficent force of fire was peculiarly in order.
And then the Greeks had another god of fire in
their benefactor *Prometheus*, who says justly of
himself in the tragedy of Aeschylus that bears
his name :

> All arts of mortals from Prometheus spring.
> [Verse 506 : tr. PLUMPTRE.]

But this fact did not lead to any conflict : the
Athenians worshipped both deities, and in similar fashion.   The central feature in the festivals
of both gods of fire was the torch race, in which
the Greek fondness for contests of all sorts was
beautifully united with the native element of
the divinities to whom worship was paid.

Trade was under the guardianship of *Hermes*,
as in a certain sense it still is to-day : the
wanderer god, whose famous staff, the caduceus
entwined with serpents, afforded security to

wanderers on the public roads, naturally also
protected the owners of caravans. But from
this point the significance of Hermes expanded
in two directions. Among the ancients, as in
our own time, trade was of two sorts : wholesale
import and export trade (*emporikē*) and local
retail trade (*kapēlikē*) ; the first enjoyed much
respect, the second very little. The fact that
Hermes extended his protection even over the
second, with its inherent knavery, could not help
lowering the significance of the god himself ; but
he stood forth in all his greatness as the guardian
of the first, which was attended by danger to
life, and as its guardian not only by land but by
sea. Here too Hermes was needed as a pro-
tector against pirates ; but more frequently the
merchant sailor was exposed to danger from the
sea itself—and therefore he prayed zealously to
all its deities, of whom I have spoken above.

And since, in consequence of the geographical
structure of the Greek territory, trade by sea
was far more important than trade by land, the
work of the merchant was hardly distinguished
from the *work of the sailor*. In Hellas its range
was immense ; Hesiod's *Works and Days* is
concerned solely with agriculture and seafaring.
And similarly in the organization of the Greek
festival seafaring is of most importance next to
agriculture. Of course the most suitable times
for sailors' festivals were the beginning and the
end of the season for sea voyages, the days that

followed the spring storms and preceded those of autumn. In Athens these festivals were the Delphinia at the beginning of April and the Pyanepsia in October : both were connected with a voyage memorable for the city of Pallas, though it was not the voyage of a merchant ; that is to say, with the voyage of Theseus, and with the offering to the Minotaur on the island of Crete of seven youths and seven maidens. With trembling, their fathers and mothers had sent them forth on their way, and with trembling they awaited their return ; the ceremonies of the two festivals naturally preserved the memory of those feelings.

To-day Greece has no special season for sea-faring ; the steam engine and the compass permit us to disregard storms and cloudy skies. In ancient times it was otherwise. Yet after the November rains there followed calm, serene days, during which Posidon's toilers could return to their work and guide home the ships that had been imprisoned in foreign ports by storms. The Greek religion of nature easily found an explanation for this strange phenomenon. It comes from the fact that at this season the female of the halcyon, a bird sacred to the god of the seas, broods over its eggs in its floating nest : for its sake Posidon with his trident smooths the waves of the sea, that they may not drown the hopes of his favourite. Hence the beautiful Greek story of the ' halcyon

days ' as days of calm after a storm ; hence
also the Greek name of December, Posideon.

But let us return to the Delphinia and the
Pyanepsia. It may seem strange that these two
most important festivals of the seafaring life
are consecrated not so much to Posidon or
Hermes as to *Apollo*, a god who might seem to
have no connection with trade or with the sea.
This is undoubtedly explained by the fact that
the whole cycle of festivals, as we have already
seen, was established by the Greek communes
with the co-operation and the approval of Delphi;
the Delphic college of priests naturally secured
for its own god a leading place in the whole
cycle. This becomes especially plain in the
ceremonies of the Pyanepsia. This festival
marked something more than the close of the
season for sea voyages ; occurring as it did at the
time when work in the fields came to an end,
the Pyanepsia was in general the most important
festival of work. And the foremost of its ceremonies impresses us by its peculiar beauty and
fulness of meaning. In the solemn procession
a handsome boy, both of whose parents were
still living (*amphithalēs*), carried an olive branch
hung with fruits, cakes, and little jars of olive
oil, honey, and milk, that is to say, with gifts of
Demeter, Dionysus, and Pallas : this was the
' eiresiōne '. He carried it to the temple of
Apollo, as the god of work and of all the joy of
work. The members of the procession mean-

while sang gay songs, two of which have been
preserved : one of them runs as follows :

Eiresione brings figs, and eiresione brings loaves ;
Honey it brings in a jar, and oil to rub on our bodies,
And a strong flagon of wine, for all to go mellow to bed on.
[Cited in PLUTARCH, *Theseus*: tr. adapted
from CLOUGH.]

On this same day the eiresione was also deposited
in private houses ; and it is plain that in them
this ceremony must have originated, being
founded on the religion of Demeter rather than
on that of Apollo. The eiresione was fastened
to the wall of the house, which it was to guard
until the next year's harvest : what was later
done with it we do not know, but there are
reasons for supposing that it was burned, with
prayer, on the family hearth.

So far we have been speaking primarily of
physical work : it is self-evident, however, that
intellectual work was also accorded religious
consecration in Greece. At first its main manifestation, and in a sense the sum of it, was poetry ;
or, to speak more exactly, since we are on Greek
ground, *choreia*, or the union of poetry, music,
and the dance, the threefold germ-cell of arts
which later became distinct from one another.

The Athenians prided themselves on the fact
that the very purity of their mountain air fitted
them for intellectual work, for poetry : there,
on lofty slopes, the intellect becomes clear, the

spirit soaring ; thence is derived creative inspiration. So the goddesses of this inspiration are
the nymphs of the mountains ; ' nympholeptic '
(possessed by nymphs) is a name given to
prophets, who have received their gift of divine
insight from the daughters of wise Nature herself. The nymphs of the mountains in their
physical aspect we call oreads (from *oros*, a
mountain), but as the givers of inspiration to
poets they have preserved a more ancient name,
akin to the Latin *mons*, the name of *Muses*.
Attica had its own ' mount of the Muses ' ; here,
according to a local tradition, they were even
said to have ' been born ', as daughters of Har-
monia ; but this tradition was no match for
older accounts, consecrated by the names of
Homer and Hesiod, according to which the
Muses, daughters of Mnemosyne (' Memory '),
dwelt either on Olympus (Homer), or on Helicon
(Hesiod). Nearer to us, however, is the Athenian
mount of the Muses, despite the fact that it later
was forced to change its name for the honoured
but unsonorous name of Philopappus, who in
the second century after Christ adorned it with
a monument which is still partially preserved.
From it there is a most marvellous view of the
Acropolis and the city of Pallas, and it is pleasant,
strolling in the cool of the evening over its
barren summit, to pray to its forgotten goddesses,
who here once on a time gave inspiration to
Aeschylus, Sophocles, and Euripides.

The Muses had under their protection all branches of man's intellectual work—*amousos*, ' deserted by the Muses ', was the term applied to those who were incapable of such work. ' Let it not be my fate to live among the *amousoi* ', was once the prayer of Euripides. The Muses bestowed their protection on man from his first uncertain steps as a child, from the time that he began to learn to read and write : in the school-room there always stood a statue of the Muse ; with her scroll or tablets in her hand she stood before the little boy's eyes as a model of the difficult art in which he was receiving instruction. And it is no wonder that he dedicated his first success to her in particular, by learning to decline her holy name before any other : *Mousa, Mousēs* in Greek grammar, *Musa, Musae* in Latin, were the examples of the ' first declension '. (And, if one be curious to inquire, that is how grammar became the most chivalrous of the sciences, including feminine nouns in the first declension and reserving masculines for the second.) In the Christian epoch such giving of honour to a pagan goddess evidently came to be regarded as inadmissible. *Musa* in grammar had to give way to the similar, but indifferent *mensa*—such is progress !

If the boy, on growing up, dedicated himself to intellectual work, the Muses became his guardians to an even greater degree. With their guardianship of the poets every one is familiar :

during the good old days of the ancient religion
they always invoked the Muses before devoting
themselves to their art—in modern times the
once living name of the Muses has become a
mere classical ghost. With them they united
other deities of joy : Apollo, Hermes, and
Pallas (to this last goddess, whom they identified
with their own Minerva, the Romans gave
special attention)—but the Muses always occupied the foremost position. And not only in
poetry—*music* received its name from them,
and these two arts, together with the dance,
received the name of the ' musical ' arts, in
distinction from the plastic arts, which developed
from handicrafts.   And when Ptolemy Soter in
the third century before Christ founded in
Alexandria the first academy of which we
have record, he with good reason called it the
Mouseion, a name which in a more limited sense
is still preserved in our ' museum '.

But one may inquire whether intellectual
work also received consecration at the Greek
religious solemnities, and if so, then where ?
It did receive it, I reply ; it received it at all of
them. It became their adornment, the principal
reason why they were not merely an occasion
for repose, but were also an educative school
for the entire nation. But with this matter
I shall deal in my next chapter.

Here in conclusion I should like to draw attention to a certain fact which is immediately

connected with the topic that we are now discussing, the consecration of work. I greatly regret that the brevity of the present sketch does not permit me to describe in somewhat more detail the ceremonies of even the most important Greek festivals, and in particular of those of Athens; the reader would then be convinced that thanks to them the Greek religion fully deserves the name of the first and only *religion of joy* in the history of humanity. This was already clear to one of her wisest sons, Pericles; in his famous funeral oration he thus expresses himself concerning that side of the life of Athens: ' We have not forgotten to provide for our weary spirits many relaxations from toil ; we have regular games and sacrifices throughout the year ; at home the style of our life is refined ; and the delight which we daily feel in all these things helps to banish melancholy ' (Thucydides, ii. 38 : tr. Jowett).

The details, I repeat, I cannot give here. But from the few data and allusions that he has encountered in this chapter the reader must already have drawn the conclusion that the Greek festivals or *holidays* had nothing in common with what we usually associate with the idea of a holiday, that is, with inactivity. In general accord with the positive character of his ethics, the Greek was organically incapable of seeing any merit in inactivity ; for him, on the contrary, a holiday was a day of intense

work, yet not of work for gain, but for the glory
of the gods and for the exaltation of his own soul.
On the day when the people were worshipping
their goddess Pallas on the Acropolis, or wit-
nessing a tragedy of Sophocles in the theatre
of Dionysus, there was obviously no room for
everyday work ; of necessity the merchant
closed his shop because he had no hope of
attracting a purchaser to it, and general indig-
nation would have descended on an archon who
had ventured to call together a jury to consider
a case in court.   But this interruption of daily
work was only the consequence of the holiday,
not its sense and inner content.   And if the
Greeks of their flourishing epoch had heard that
there existed or ever would exist a people who
beheld in work as such an offence to the holiday
and to the worship of their god, an offence which
even deserved to be ' rooted out '—they would
have come to the conclusion that that people had
extremely strange notions of piety.

Obviously a time came even for them when
they renounced this conviction : were they the
better for it ?   The question requires no answer ;
the most hasty comparison of even the mere
external appearance of ancient Greece and of
Byzantine Greece will answer it most eloquently.

IV

THE REVELATION OF GOD IN BEAUTY

EACH deity dwells in its proper element and spiritualizes it : such was probably the oldest conception of the Greeks as of other nations. I will call it *animatism*, thus somewhat modifying, in order to make it more fruitful, the meaning of this term, which was introduced by the anthropologist Marett. At first the deity was merged with its element, not possessing a form independent of it ; this was the period of *immanent* animatism. But gradually the concentration of thought and feeling on the deity itself, as the soul of the element, led to its being physically distinguished from the element : a dryad might remain in her tree, but she might also leave it, though she remained near at hand as *its* dryad. The period of *transcendent* animatism began. Then for distinction the deity required its own form, separate from the form of the element : of what sort then was that form to be?

This is a decisive, a fatal question.

The passage to transcendent animatism is not peculiar to the Greek religion, it is a usual phenomenon ; the answer to the question of

form is characteristic of each religion. It is
evident that a form of any sort can be no more
than a symbol, for the gods are essentially invisible and reveal themselves only to whom they
wish and when they wish. How then shall the
invisible be expressed in visible form ? How
and in what does the god reveal himself ? In
strength, some reply ; in a mysteriousness full of
meaning, others reply; in appalling hideousness,
still others reply. Thus the Hindu represents his
god with many arms ; the Egyptian gives to his
god the head of a jackal, an ibis, or the like ;
the imagination of a savage pictures his god with
a distorted visage and with protruding tusks.
Only the Greek replied : ' God reveals himself
in *beauty*.'

After all, he could make absolutely no other
reply: nowhere in the world is there a land so
beautiful as Hellas. If even to-day it enchants
its still infrequent guests—to-day, when its
inhabitants, after depriving nature of divinity,
have stripped from her her green garment of
forests and have dried up the silver streams of
the rivers—then in what form must we imagine
it in the happy times of peace and of love between
Mother Earth and men her children ? No, the
deities which gave life to this nature could not help
being beautiful themselves ; it sufficed to be conscious of her beauty in order to have the single
appropriate answer arise of its own accord.

But for this, obviously, time was required ;

even the Greeks conducted their deity through
imperfect stages of strength, horror, and suggest-
iveness, before they found truly divine relief
in beauty. And since an image formed in dusky
ages may be preserved, thanks to a feeling of
piety, up to the latest times—for the brutal
tendency to iconoclasm was organically foreign
to the Greek—therefore even in the historic
epoch one might encounter a four-armed Apollo
in Laconia, a Demeter with a horse's head in
Arcadia, and in particular—horribly hideous
Erinyes and Gorgons. But these were merely
scattered phenomena. Men were disturbed by
these traits least in the Erinyes, the Gorgons,
and the like ; that is, in personifications of dark,
malicious forces ; Aeschylus was still content
with them. But towards the end of the fifth
century the general tendency towards beauty
overcame the survival, which might have seemed
fully justified. No, a higher force cannot be
hideous. It may be terrible, if need be ; but
cannot beauty be terrible ? And so the later
types of the Erinyes and Gorgons were created,
pale, grim—and beautiful ; the blood runs cold
in our veins at the glance of this Medusa (the
' Medusa Rondanini ')—and yet we feel that we
have before us an unearthly beauty. Only one
god remained, by exception, in his beastlike
ugliness, withstanding the victorious assault of
the new beauty ; though others might be transformed, *Pan* could not be separated from his

goatish form.   But he remained isolated among
the fair Grecian Olympians.   The Greeks themselves showed a good-natured toleration of the
fact ; but when Christian times came the goat-
legged god passed for ever into the new plastic
mythology under the name of the devil.

But let us not make too great haste.   Even
then, when the thought of the Greeks had
found the single divine answer to the question
of the external form of the god, they were still
far from giving it perfect expression : the chisel
and the brush could not keep pace with creative
thought ; the bonds that restrained them were
too powerful.   Even in that primitive epoch
connected with the name of Daedalus, the
artist doubtless desired to give to the divine
form, up to the measure of his strength, the
beauty that hovered before his eyes ; but his
hand reluctantly followed his will; the image
that he produced was childishly imperfect.   And
yet the reverence with which it was regarded
by contemporaries, who evidently saw in it a
model of perfection, passed from generation to
generation, down to later times more skilled in
art.   Great was the danger of stagnation :
' originals ' might have been created with a
monopoly of sanctity, and the sculptors of divine
forms in mature times might have felt themselves restrained by them.   Then the vision of
beauty would have flown away anew, without
attaining its final realization.

Great was the triumph of the Greek genius that overcame this danger. Of course the ' Daedalid ' statues of the gods with their naïve conventionalism remained in the old temples : the son did not refuse worship to what his father worshipped ; tradition renewed its sanctifying force. And if by chance a fire destroyed them, then the love of the worshippers, inherited from times of old, strove to reproduce them as far as possible in the same form—this was the condition for preserving that same feeling. Thus arose so-called ' archaistic ' statues, large numbers of which have been preserved. But nothing restrained an artist from making a statue of the same god for a *new* temple of the god in the form most perfect according to his own conception ; the two currents, the conservative and the progressive, flowed on side by side, not in the least hampering each other.

In the sixth century before Christ an ideal of beauty had already been attained in the making of images of the gods, an ideal that remains such even for us : the Pre-Raphaelites have taught us to appreciate the innocent charm of this so-called ' ripe archaic '. Yet individualization was lacking. Of course nobody could mistake Posidon for Apollo or the reverse : the beard or the lack of it settled the question. But yet the gods were like one another and like men ; we distinguish them only by their attributes :

the trident characterizes Posidon ; the wand
with serpents, Hermes ; the thunderbolt, Zeus ;
the lion's skin, Heracles ; and so on.

This was still imperfection ; following generations, in the fifth and fourth centuries, were
successful in overcoming it.   We shall ill appreciate Phidias, Alcamenes, and Praxiteles, if we
see in them only artists, even of religious sculpture : they were genuine prophets, prophets of
the chisel.   The same work which the prophets
of the Old Testament performed for ancient
Israel—the creation of a clear-cut, lofty, and at
the same time harmonious conception of deity—
that same work artists performed for the ancient
Hellenes, and, moreover, so much the more
successfully as an image is more powerful than
a word.   On a dogmatic and narrative basis the
creation of unity was impossible : there was no
central organ which possessed the strength or
even—for we are in Greece—the desire to annihi-
late everything that opposed it ; ceremonial rites
therefore differed widely in different states.   But
from the moment that Phidias created his *Zeus*
of Olympia it was impossible to imagine the god
in any other form.   Yes, that was verily he, a
god majestic but kindly, ' father of gods and
men ' ; such indeed was he at the moment when
he promised the mother who embraced his knees
that he would fulfil her prayer :

He spoke, and under his dark brows the nod
Vouchsafed of confirmation.   All around

The Sovereign's everlasting head his curls
Ambrosial shook, and huge Olympus reeled.
      [*Iliad*, i. 528-530 : tr. adapted from COWPER.]

And evidently, in the face of this majestic
beauty, all petty and vulgar conceptions with
which intellectual immaturity or the caprice of
poets had defiled the image of the Olympian
must vanish away like smoke ; with it there
were in harmony only the most noble, the most
majestic, the most Aeschylean ideas :

Weighing all other names I fail to guess
Aught else but Zeus, if I would cast aside,
      Clearly, in very deed,
From off my soul this idle weight of care.
      [AESCHYLUS, *Agamemnon*, 163-166, ed. Weil :
                              tr. PLUMPTRE.]

And never again could a man be completely
unhappy, to whom the lord of the world had
once revealed himself in his Olympian form.

Yet with all its graciousness, his was a stern
beauty. Still sterner was his spouse, the Argive
Hera of Polyclitus, the contemporary of Phidias, Hera the Fulfiller, the guardian of the
sacrament of marriage for Grecian women, of
marriage with its stern duties to which the
careless freedom of a maiden's life must give
place. And equally stern was the Athena
revealed to his nation by Phidias, Athena the
Maiden, denizen of the Parthenon that was
named in her honour, who pointed out to an
Athenian his duties as a warrior and a citizen,

but who also, in return for the performance of
these duties, defended his country by her prayers
before the throne of her mighty father, as Solon,
the ancient lawgiver of Athens, had said of her :

> Our city everlastingly shall stand ;
> So Zeus and all the immortal gods command :
> Athenian Pallas lends her heavenly aid,
> She of the mighty father, heavenly maid.
>   [Cited by DEMOSTHENES, *On the Embassy*, 254 :
>   tr. adapted from KENNEDY.]

This sternness was decidedly mitigated in the
figure of *Demeter*, the mother-goddess, the kindly
nourisher and comforter of man ; we do not
know to whom we owe the statue that became
her type, but one kindred to it in expression has
been preserved to us in a good copy, the statue of
Irene, the beneficent goddess of peace, modelled
near the beginning of the fourth century by
the sculptor Cephisodotus. It begins the new
epoch of religious sculpture which followed the
Peloponnesian War, the epoch of the younger
prophets, who revealed to the Greeks and to
ourselves the nature of their subordinate and
younger gods. At the head of these sculptors
stand Praxiteles and Lysippus. At this time
three beautiful types of youthful god were
created. Only one of them has been preserved
to us in the original of its creator, Praxiteles, but
its superiority to all copies makes us conceive
of the two others as equally perfect. *Apollo*,
with his form of more than earthly slenderness

and lightness, was the ideal of bright beauty of
intellect, the incarnation of spirit, reverie, and
will. *Dionysus*, full of melancholy dreaming,
was the god of the hidden charm of nature,
attractive but mysterious, like the damp breath
of spring with its tidings of awakening, of the
coming of life-giving strength. *Hermes* was
elastic youthful strength, the incarnation of
action and reality, but of reality as it should
be, not as it is.

By their side stood two young female types.
Aphrodite, the queen of the charm of love, was
the justification of life-giving sensuousness in
the purity of beauty. I beg the reader not to
think so much of the famous ' Medicean Venus ',
which already has a faint odour of the court
licence of Alexandrianism (in consequence of
which it so perfectly suited the taste of the classicism of the gallants of the seventeenth century)
as of the Aphrodite of Praxiteles, despite the
serious imperfection of the copy of it in the
Vatican. She corresponds to Dionysus. In the
same fashion, to Hermes corresponds *Artemis*,
the divine huntress, strong and agile, as befits a
goddess who knows no rest in coursing through
the woods and glades, or in dancing by night at
the head of a chorus of Dryads. *Pallas* would
have corresponded to Apollo, had not her type
been already settled by the religious sculpture of
the preceding epoch ; and after all the well-
known ' Pallas Giustiniani ' may have been an

approximation of the ideal of Phidias to the
more earthly tendencies of the fourth century.
The loftiness of the conceptions of Phidias and
Polyclitus did not exclude such transformations :
the Olympian Zeus and the Argive Hera were
likewise subject to them ; and the busts of Zeus
(' Otricoli ') and of Hera (' Ludovisi '), which all
my readers know, and which aroused the well-
founded enthusiasm of Winckelmann and of
Goethe, are really just such justified metamorphoses in the spirit of the religio-artistic needs
of the fourth century.

Posidon was the own brother of Zeus ; but
beside him he was what the sea, full of stormy
motion, is in comparison with the majestic calm
of the sky.   Lysippus understood this ; in his
Posidon he expressed just this quality of stormy
violence.   Though the face of his Posidon
is like that of Zeus, yet it lacks the calm
' nodding of the brows' of the ruler of Olympus ;
his brows are raised threateningly, as is his hair
also ; his whole figure is the strength of a
raging wave incarnate in a divine form.   The
' true son of Zeus ' was *Heracles*, born a mortal ;
but earthly sufferings left their stamp on him,
and so created a veritable tragedy of divine man-
hood.   Sophocles expressed this in poetry,
Lysippus in sculpture.   (Witness the ' Farnese
Heracles '.)

Finally, in the third century, this same image
of the Zeus of Phidias went through one more

transformation and produced, under the chisel
of Bryaxis, the last work of Greek religious
sculpture, the Sarapis of Alexandria ; by this
purely Greek deity Ptolemy wished to replace
for the Greeks of his kingdom the Egyptian
Osiris, the brother and husband of Isis.   Thus
did Bryaxis understand him, as Zeus of the underworld, the brother of the torch-bearing Demeter
of the Eleusinian mysteries, for the Greeks had
originally represented Isis in the form of Demeter.
Zeus, Posidon, and Sarapis are as it were three
brothers, the rulers of the sky, the sea, and the
kingdom of the underworld.   The curls of Zeus
rise and fall in a waving line ; the mane of
Posidon bristles stormily ; the skeins of the hair
of Sarapis droop sadly, casting a dark shadow
on his serene brow.

I have reserved till the last one more transformation of this same Zeus of Phidias, though
it was of earlier date than Bryaxis : I mean
Asclepius.   This healer of men, their saviour
from inexorable death, was goodness personified ;
the period of the special flourishing of his cult,
in his capacity as saviour, began about the time
of the birth of Christ.

Before we go further, let us cast a backward
glance.

That the race of the Olympians, created by the
great Greek artists and incorporated in marble
and bronze, was a genuine 'revelation of divinity

in beauty ', has been felt by other men besides
ourselves, to whom, if we except the Olympian
Hermes of Praxiteles, not one of those incorpora-
tions has come down in the original.   If even the
copies that have survived and that are preserved
in our museums have drawn from a historian
of the Christian religion the ecstatic exclama-
tion, ' Very gods, very goddesses ! ' (Renan)—
then how must the ' riginals themselves have
acted on the nation for which they were created !
As a matter of fact, even the sober and discreet
Aristotle testifies : ' Doubtless if men differed
from one another in the mere forms of their
bodies as much as the statues of the gods do
from men, all would acknowledge that the
inferior class should be slaves of the superior '
(*Politics*, i. 5, 10 : tr. Jowett).

Here we have what was a stumbling-block,
and in the opinion of many men still is so : the
ancient Greeks worshipped their statues, served
them ; their cult was ' idolatry '.

Some go still further : pointing to fragmentary
forms of this idolatry, which show that in dim
ages before the appearance of statues in human
form, primitive blocks of all sorts likewise
served as objects of worship, they speak of
' fetishism ' in the religion of ancient Greece.
Excellent : now we have a common religious
foundation for the Greeks and for the savages of
Upper and Lower Guinea.

First let us examine ' fetishism '. When

Portuguese sailors, who in their own country
worshipped the Lord Jesus, the Mother of God,
and the saints on the canvases of their great
masters, became acquainted with the formless
blocks of the savages whom I have just mentioned, they gave them the name *feitiço*, or
facticius (*deus*), that is ' (god) made with hands ',
for the reason that in their opinion (whether
correct or not is a matter of no consequence)
the given tribe of savages beheld in such a block
not an image or symbol of a deity existing outside it and independent of it, but the deity itself.
Otherwise we should have to term fetishists
even the Christians, and not only the Catholics
and the Orthodox, but also the Protestants,
who admit that the crucifix is something holy ;
or else the very term ' fetishism ' would lose all
value as the expression of an idea, and would
retain value only—as an insult.

And now I inquire : Have we any right to
suppose that for King Minos and his subjects
the *labrys* (a double-bladed axe) was not the
symbol of Zeus, the caster of thunderbolts, but
an independent deity, and that the stonecutter
who drew the outline of it on the wall regarded
himself as ' making a god ' ? Evidently the
dumb memorial can tell us nothing as to the
attitude of men towards it.   Therefore we
must judge according to the analogy of later
ages ; that is, we must pass from ' fetishism '
to ' idolatry '.

Here the matter is absolutely clear, from
Homer onward. When Zeus promises Thetis
that he will fulfil her prayer, when Athena fills
the heart of Diomedes with ardour and with
valour, when Apollo protects Hector, what have
we before us, gods acting by their own free will,
or statues made by the hand of man ? The
question is superfluous, the more so since
the Achaean epoch, represented by Homer,
knew absolutely no statues. But perhaps in
the following epoch, which built temples to the
gods and placed their statues in them, there
ensued a transformation of religious feeling
and in the consciousness of the faithful the
statues took the place of the gods that they
were meant to represent ? Let us see. A
throng of many thousand Athenians is gathered
in the theatre to witness the *Oresteia* of Aeschylus ; it sees how the hero, pursued by the
Erinyes, embraces with his arms the *statue* of
Pallas on the Acropolis ; later on Pallas *herself*
descends to him and thus stands beside her
statue. Can one not clearly see from this that
the statue is only the image of the deity, and not
the deity itself ?

Yet the Greeks bowed down to their statues.
To be sure ; but absolutely in the same sense in
which faithful followers of the old Christian faiths
' bow down ' (the phrase is of no importance here)
to the images of Christ, the Mother of God, and
the saints ; and an Athenian who burned incense

before the statue of his Pallas, did so with
absolutely the same feeling with which to-day
a Catholic or an Orthodox Christian on Saturday
evening lights a lamp before the image of the
Most Holy Virgin. And as now the faithful
distinguish ' miraculous ' images from others,
and ascribe to them greater sanctity, just so, in
absolutely the same way, the statue of Apollo
in Magnesia on the Meander was believed to
have ' power for all things '. Here the analogy
is complete, nor is there anything strange in
the fact, for here we are dealing with the ancient
foundation of Christianity. On the other hand,
it is true that for that very reason the Protestants cannot deny themselves the pleasure of
calling *us* ' idolaters ' ; but we know nevertheless that, when they speak thus, they merely
invent charges against us, and do not argue
seriously.

Thanks to the Christian apologists, the
reproach of idolatry cleaved to the ancient
Greek religion. Christian apologetics in its
turn followed after Jewish apologetics, which
had its own iconoclastic leaven in the revelations of the Prophets of the Old Testament, but
which in its dispute with Hellenism merely
repeated the arguments of the Greek philosophical apologetics of the Epicureans, the New
Academicians, and the Cynics. In them two
arguments were of chief importance.

The first, which is characteristic of philoso-

phical apologetics, pertains to anthropomorphism
in general, as the foundation not only of the
worship of statues, but of their very existence.
It dates from Xenophanes, the rhapsodist and
philosopher of the sixth century before Christ.
' The Ethiopians,' he said, ' represent their
gods as black, and if horses had the power to
make statues of their gods, they would give them
the form of a horse ' (Fragments, 15, 16: Diels).
And what of it ? We, men of the twentieth
century, and others as well, may reply to this
argument with the immortal words of Goethe,
' All that is transitory is naught but a parable '
(*Faust*, Part II., near close), and we may add
that even religion itself, as the reflection of the
deity in the consciousness of transitory man, is
something transitory, is naught but a parable.
Let us inquire of Aeschylus what he would reply
to Xenophanes. ' O Zeus—whoe'er he be, if
that name please him well, by that on him I
call ' (*Agamemnon*, 160-162, ed. Weil: tr.
adapted from Plumptre), said the prophet of
Eleusis, rightly emphasizing the Hellenic feeling
of the relativity of our gods, which differed so
widely from Semitic exclusiveness. And doubtless in the same spirit he would also have replied
to Xenophanes : ' O Zeus, of *whatever nature*
thou art, if it please thee that we worship thee
in this form, in this form do we worship thee ! '
—in a form created, let us assume, by Antenor,
and later by Phidias.

But whence did all the Greeks know what was dear to Zeus ? Of that we shall speak later.

As a matter of fact it is highly probable that Xenophanes had no need of any such instruction ; we have only fragments of his work preserved. It is highly probable that the Greek rhapsodist did not object to the worship of statues, but to the identification of their transitory form with the eternal form of the deity, independent of human feelings. But, I repeat, this whole argument is characteristic only of Hellenico-philosophic apologetics ; the Jews, and after them the Christians, who admitted that God created man ' in his image, after his likeness ', obviously could not avail themselves of it.

Another argument is more popular. The Greek worships a statue, hence the work of a stonecutter or a founder. He ascribes to man the power of making a god. What an absurdity! Here, I will take and break off the arm of your god ; let us see whether he will be able to defend himself and to punish me. And you, blind men, instead of worshipping the work of a man, should worship rather the being who created the man himself, your human god-maker.

This argument is apparently very convincing— and it has shown its force in practice, in dark times and against dark men ; but we, Athenians of the fourth and third centuries, see it as it really is, a piece of fundamentally false reasoning, sometimes instinctive, but more often blended with duplicity. We really worship Pallas in the form which Phidias has created for her, but never have we ascribed to her statue the power of self-defence against the blow of a barbarian. If you maim her statue, it will be sacrilege, a sin of the same sort as perjury, disrespect for your parents, or injury to a guest ; and you may be sure that the goddess will punish you for it—if not at once, then at some time in the future ; if not in this world, then in the next world ; if not in your own person, then in the person of your descendants down to the fourth generation and beyond. And apart from that, your act will be an offence to our religious feeling, for which we will punish you in our own name, and at once. As for your expression ' the god-maker ', that is a piece of vulgar ignorance on your part. Never will a statue, not even one formed by Phidias himself, be an object of worship for its own sake : while it remains in the artist's workshop he himself and any other man may cut it, may break off what parts he pleases, may even pound it into bits, and that will not be sacrilege. *A statue becomes an object of worship only at the moment of consecration (hidrysis)*, that is, through a religious ceremony of a sacramental character and of great solemnity, of which you may read in the *Exegetics* of Autoclides. The consecration itself must be preceded by an invocation of the god with an inquiry whether he is pleased with the statue which we consecrate to him, and whether he consents to infuse into it a portion of his divine power, in order that henceforth it may be a visible mediator between him, the invisible, and his worshippers. In ordinary cases it suffices to address with this aim in view the local 'exegete' of the Pythian Apollo or the Eleusinian goddesses; on more solemn occasions we send an embassy to Delphi.

But Phidias, when he framed his Olympian Zeus, ventured to address the Cloudgatherer himself with the query whether he was pleased with his statue, and from the heights of the heavens the god cast a thunderbolt, his fiery messenger, at the artist's feet. Journey to Olympia : there they will show you the holy *enēlysion*, the place where smote the thunderbolt of Zeus, bringing joy to us and eternal glory to his prophet.

Let us proceed. Hitherto I have been speaking of only one form of artistic revelation, of sculpture ; and of that in only one field, in the field of creating statues as objects of worship. I must here remark that in this connection painting is subordinate : paintings of the gods, as objects of worship, are not found at all in the public cult, and but rarely in the private cults. I shall speak later of painting, and of the other branches of sculpture ; at present I have a word to say of *architecture*.

In those distant times of the ' Achaean epoch ', when statues of the gods were unknown, temples were also dispensed with ; divine service in the name of the state was celebrated under the open sky, and required an altar, but no temple.   The temple developed only gradually, along with the need for a dwelling, of course not for the invisible god, but for his visible form, the statue.   Such a temple was most likely an outgrowth and development of the sacred grove ; as, for example, was the earliest form of the temple of Delphi recorded by Pausanias.   At first men formed an arbour by intertwining its trees, thus providing a shelter for the statue (this custom, which is mentioned by Homer, was preserved in some cults down to the latest times) ; later they thought it more secure to build a small house among the trees, and finally they transformed this house and the trees that surrounded it into a building wholly or in part of stone : thus arose the cella and its colonnade, the form of ' Greek temple ' that we all know, simple but majestic and enchanting.   Divine service was celebrated as of old at an altar under the open sky, *in front of* the temple, and not in the temple, which was only the habitation of the deity, and not a place for assemblies of the faithful.   Therefore there was no need for building temples of any great size ; even the most magnificent among them were of modest dimensions in comparison with the stone giants of the oriental religions and of Christianity.

Where were the temples built ? When the
rule of kings came to an end in the Greek states,
their acropoleis were transformed from royal
citadels into natural tabernacles of the gods ;
on them, for the most part, the temples were
erected. Thus in Athens, on the Acropólis,
the temple of Pallas occupied the site of the
' house of Erechtheus ' of Achaean times, and
inherited its name ; and by its side arose other
temples of the same goddess, culminating in the
Parthenon. Moreover, temples were very desirable in the market-place, where matters of state
were decided. The centres of universal Hellenic
religious feeling, the sacred groves at Delphi and
at Olympia, were full of temples. The Greeks
also liked to build them on the highways, outside
the city walls, like the churches *fuori le mura* in
Christian Rome, that a traveller might experience
from afar the joyous feeling of approach to a city
where reigned ' good order ' (*eunomia*). A still
more desirable place was a promontory visible
from afar to sailors—even to-day a pilgrim who
sails past the Attic promontory of Sunium with
the white columns of its temple to Posidon,
may experience the same warm feeling of inti-
mate divine favour that this temple once aroused
in the citizens and guests of Athens.

All these were temples in the highest sense of
the term. To complete our picture of the external aspect of Hellenic religion we must include
the chapels of the nymphs and local heroes, small

and unpretentious, but marvellous in their very
simplicity, which inspired meditation ; nor must
we forget the grottos and sacred groves, and the
modest figures of the rural gods.   Here a thyrsus,
resting against a fig tree of strange form, or a
tympanum hung upon a bough, marked a tree as
consecrated to Dionysus ; there a herm of Pallas
peered forth from the hole of an olive tree ;
there again a boundary column was crowned
by the head of Hermes or of Pan.   Everywhere
was an appropriate mingling of nature with art
in a general harmony of religious feeling such as
Mother Earth has seen but once in her long life.
A man of to-day may gain an idea of it from the
Pompeian painted landscapes, especially those
small and modest landscapes which are not widely
known and which do not at once attract the
attention of visitors to the ruins of the dumb
city and the halls of the museum at Naples.

Sculpture, to which I now return, lent its aid
here also : sculpture adorned the temple which
served as the dwelling of the god which a sculptor
had created.   If the temple as a whole, in
accordance with the leading principle of Greek
tectonics, was a natural and yet beautiful
expression of the work of constructive forces,
sculpture adorned the repose which ensued upon
this work, that is, the flat places in which the
opposing forces counterbalanced each other.
Such were the pediment, the flat triangle of the
façade between the horizontal line of the cornice

and the copings of the roof, and the metopes, or quadrangles of the frieze between the triglyphs which supported the cornice. Here there was room for whole groups of statuary, large on the pediments, small on the metopes. And each group of statuary gave an opportunity for the portrayal of mythology, that poetic religion which is not binding on the faithful, which is just as beautiful as the citizen's religion but still subordinate to it. So let the chisel carve on the pediments scenes of the birth of Pallas and of her dispute with Posidon over the Attic land, or scenes of the contests of Pelops and Oenomaüs and of the rape of the women of the Lapithae by the wild Centaurs : nobody is obliged to believe that all this took place as represented, or that it ever took place at all. But the contemplation of these beautiful white figures on the dark, painted background fills us with a spirit of majestic beauty, and through it with the spirit of religion.

Finally, the votive offerings. They crowded the ' cella ', the vestibules, the spaces between the columns, the steps of the temple, and its near vicinity : statues, bas-reliefs, pictures, all were gathered together here. Each temple was a museum, but a museum consecrated to the glory of the deity and thereby directing anew the soul of the spectator through beauty to religion. Thus the enclosures of the gods most widely worshipped by all the Hellenes, of Apollo at

Delphi, of Demeter and Cora at Eleusis, of Pallas
on the Acropolis, and of Zeus at Olympia, were
absolute kingdoms of religious beauty and of
beautiful religion.   When one reads even the dry
catalogues of Pausanias, one's soul weeps at that
vanished beauty, filled with spirit, a beauty such
as the world was never to behold again.   And
yet Pausanias surveyed it in the second century
after Christ, after the devastations of many
pitiless wars and the plunderings of Roman
governors: what then must it have been in those
times to which our thoughts have gone back,
in the flourishing fourth and third centuries
before Christ ?

The beauty of a motionless image was only
one of two forms of the revelation of divinity ;
the second was the beauty—of word, will the
reader prompt me ?   No.   The Greek would not
have been a Greek if he had so limited the
domain subject to his Muse.   No, the second was
all beauty that is the expression of moving,
transitory feeling, not only in word, but in music,
and not only in music, but in dumb gesture.   I am
here speaking of the complete activity of the
Hellenic Muse, of the triune *choreia*, composed in
equal degree of poetry, music, and the dance.
All these arts were consecrated to the divinity,
but supreme among the three was the *dance*.

This is a matter organically incomprehensible
to the religious feeling of modern times.   For

some reason or other—whether owing to the
heavy raiment worn in oriental countries, or to
the cause of that raiment, an unnatural and
exaggerated effort to cover modestly the forms
of the body, as something essentially unclean,
or possibly owing to its own deep-rooted dislike
for visible images of all sorts—Judaism, the
negative source of Christianity, has absolutely
obliterated in the heirs of the ancient Greek
religious feeling, even their capacity for understanding this important basis of that feeling.
What man among us can thoroughly appreciate
those weighty words of Plato : ' Our young
people must not merely dance well, they must
dance good things ' ! (Abbreviated from *Laws*,
ii. 654.) In order to apprehend their sense we
need an analogy from the domain of the word :
' Not only to speak well, but to speak good
things '. And meanwhile psychology teaches us
that a gesture is far more immediate and more
convincing than a word, and logic bids us confess
that accordingly a poem of gesture—or a dance
in the proper antique meaning of the word—
if it were really created, would stir our souls far
more powerfully than the most inspired poem of
words can possibly stir them. To-day some persons, kindled with an enthusiasm derived from
antique sources, are making attempts to ' liberate
the body ', to give back to plastic gesture its
ancient rights. Though their efforts would certainly have made on the ancient Greeks the same

impression that the exercises in articulate speech
of a dumb man who is being taught to speak in
his adult years make on us, yet we should hail
them with joy and support them: perchance our
grandsons will succeed in unearthing the buried
temple, in giving back to man his lost fullness
of life.

The Greeks knew this fullness—but alas, not
even they invented any notation for the dance,
and therefore the inspired poems of the ancient
choreographers, which were imparted to others
only by means of imitative performance, have
perished for ever. We can speak only of their
significance, and how great it was we may judge
from the fact that all the greater festivals were
combined with dances of maidens, those flowers
of the race. Besides this, the young men showed
their beauty in the most diverse physical
exercises, on foot and on horseback, in light
garments or in arms; and in Athens even old men
of noble form with olive branches in their hands
marched in the procession in honour of the goddess—this was their choreia.

Music and *poetry*, as elements of the choreia
which was one element of the divine service,
are immediately intelligible even to us, owing
to the fact that our church has preserved them
and developed them. The ancient religion was
also familiar with spiritual music; it accompanied spiritual poetry, which was of extremely
varied types, and it certainly was itself equally

varied ; it was simple in its means but powerful
in its effect.   But we know very little about it.
We know best the spiritual *poetry* of the Greeks,
though even here our information is extremely
fragmentary.   Only the highest form of the
triune choreia stands before us in the full light
of history—the drama ; but again only in its
verbal, not in its musical and orchestic aspect.
The drama was the most perfect expression of
the Dionysian idea ; only on that religious
background can it be completely understood.

Our picture would be very incomplete, if, in
speaking of the choric element in the Hellenic
divine service, we did not properly emphasize a
certain feature which invariably accompanies
it—*agonistics*.   While understanding in proper
fashion the idea of equality, as a potential
equality, that is, the general accessibility of
good things in proportion to the absolutely
different talents of different men, the ancient
democracy consecrated by its religion the tendency to competition, that spur to the exertion
and the development of all individual forces for
the common good.   And it did so in the most
various forms.   We easily understand competition in gymnastic exercises ; here agonistics
is the soul of the whole matter.   Agonistics in
the choreia is less intelligible to us ; yet here too
it was an inevitable feature.   Different groups
of girls competed, engaging in choral dances ;
adults competed, noted rhapsodists, who recited

Homer at the festival of the Panathenaea ; but rhapsodists of tender years also competed, the sons of citizens, reciting Homer at the festival of the Apaturia. Tragic poets competed at the festival of Dionysus ; choruses likewise competed, executing the ' lyric ' (that is, the specifically choric) parts of the tragedy; finally, the actors who took the principal parts also competed. Nor is this all ; agonistics consecrated to a certain degree even the lower, vulgar forms of popular merriment : at the Rural Dionysia a prize was given to the man who could stand longest on one bare foot on a full wine skin smeared with olive oil ; at the Anthesteria to the man who could first, at a sign given by a herald, empty a tankard of wine.

To be sure, similar things happen among us, also, wherever popular merrymakings are held. But here is something that excites amazement. A recently discovered fragment of Herodas informs us of the *agōn eupaidiās* on the last day of the Thesmophoria : a prize was given to the happy mother who had given birth to the most beautiful child during the year. The details of the matter are unknown, but the fact is established.

The most beautiful—even here Hellas remained faithful to herself. And at the festival of Demeter Thesmophoros, Demeter the Lawgiver. For *god reveals himself in beauty*—such is the faith of the Hellene, blasphemously forgotten by his heirs.

V

THE CONSECRATION OF HUMAN SOCIETY

WE are now passing to those aspects of Greek religion that have been termed ' higher '—though a certain apostasy from Mother Earth was necessary in order to call them such in distinction from those that we have discussed previously. We must first speak of the religious consecration of human society : or, on the one hand, of the family, the clan, and the tribe ; on the other, of the group and corporation ; and further, of the city, the state, Hellas, humanity.

The central element of the *family*, that germ-cell of a society of citizens, which was bound together by possessing one common roof, was constituted by a divine being, the *household hearth*. The depth of the religious feeling of the Greeks expressed itself in the fact that for them (and apparently for them only) this was a being of feminine gender, the goddess *Hestia*. While she is one of the oldest deities, she changes before our very eyes, one may say, from an immanent deity, such as she is in Homer, to a transcendent deity. For Hesiod she is already an individual goddess, the sister of Zeus, like Hera and Demeter ; but in contrast to them she is a maiden : that is because her element is the flame of fire. The late date of her change to a transcendent deity caused images of her to be infrequent : even in the public temples no statues were erected to her, and she was worshipped in her symbol, the undying fire on the altar within the temple. In the house the case was evidently the same.

Having a constant abode on the hearth that was consecrated to her, Hestia was a true symbol of the mistress of the house, whose activity, as distinguished from the activity of her husband, went on within the house ; immediate bonds united Hestia with the house-mistress. And while, in consequence of the ' patrilinear ' organization of the Greek family, the house and all other possessions normally passed from father to son, and the children took their names from the name of the father, for Hestia matrilinear succession was the law. When a young wife was conducted to the house of her husband, her mother walked in front with a torch that had been lighted at the hearth of *her* house, and with this torch she lighted a new fire on the hearth of her daughter and son-in-law—a beautiful symbol of all that household tradition which thenceforward was to pass from the mother through

the daughter, the young mistress, into the new
house.   Thus conducted into the house, Hestia
becomes its goddess-protectress, potent and
gracious.   Of the intimacy and the heartfelt
character of this relation we have testimony in
the moving prayer spoken by Alcestis before
her death, in the play of Euripides :

> She . . . before Hestia's altar stood, and prayed :
> ' Queen, for I pass beneath the earth, I fall
> Before thee now, and nevermore, and pray :—
> Be mother to my orphans : mate with him
> A loving wife, with her a noble husband.
> Nor, as their mother dieth, so may they,
> My children, die untimely, but with weal
> In the home-land fill up a life of bliss.'
>   [*Alcestis*, 162-169 : tr. adapted from WAY.]

In return for these benefactions she was regarded with great honour.   In prayers addressed
to many gods it was the custom to mention
her first : ' Hestia, from whom reason bids us
begin ', says the old king in the *Phaëthon* of
the same Euripides (Fragment 781 : Nauck);
the expression, ' to begin from Hestia ', even
became proverbial.   The master of the house
prayed to her when he started on a journey, and
he greeted her when he returned home.   When
a child was born in the house, it was carried
round the hearth on the fifth day, more or less,
and was thus presented to Hestia ; this was a
genuine family festival (the Amphidromia), in
which all present at the birth of the child took

part ; it was accompanied by a banquet. Every
one who sat by the hearth (*ephestios*) was holy ;
by this act a fugitive could ordinarily secure the
protection of the man to whom he turned for
help.

Just as Hestia was the female element of a
family, so its male element was *Zeus of the Garth*
(*Zeus Herkeios*), who stood beside his altar in
the courtyard. Here took place the household
sacrifices, conducted by the master of the house :
before the sacrifice he plunged a burning brand
from the altar into a pail of water and with this
consecrated water sprinkled all present, both
members of the household and guests, both freemen and slaves. This *sprinkling* (*chernips*) was
a sacramental act, strengthening the bonds that
united those present ; therefore exclusion from
the ceremony of sprinkling was a punishment
visited on godless men. The sacrifice was
combined with a banquet, and may even be said
to have mainly depended on it : in honour of
the god there were burned only symbolic por-
tions of the sacrificed beast, such as had little
value for food ; the remainder was consumed
by the invited guests, who thus became ' fellow-
banqueters of the gods '. The Greeks understood perfectly that a god needed worship,
expressed by a symbol, and not material food ;
therefore the annihilation of a sacrificial animal
by a ' holocaust ' was not one of their customs.
On the other hand, the scarcity of animal food

caused every slaying of a beast to be accompanied by a sacrifice, so that even our word to
slaughter (an animal) had as its Greek correspondent ' to make a sacrifice of ' (*hiereuein, thyein*),
a term which also certainly gave expression to
the delicacy of feeling on which I have commented
above (p. 45).

Other gods, varying in different circumstances,
might of course also be guardians of the house ;
the *spirits of the ancestors* of the master ordinarily
had this function.   This again is one of the sides
of Greek religion most closely connected with
household life.   The spirits of the ancestors live ;
the master of the house bestows on them the
gifts and liquid offerings hallowed by custom ;
they are therefore concerned that his family
may prosper and may preserve the purity of its
blood, of *their* blood. From their habitation
beneath the earth the spirits of the ancestors
' send aloft good ' to their descendant ;   the
living invite them to take part in the joy of the
marriage feast, which is their joy to an equal
degree ; and it is no wonder that they pursue
with implacable wrath the sinful wife who,
breaking her vow of conjugal fidelity, has
interrupted the hereditary continuity of their
blood and has introduced ' falsified children '
to them and into her house. And since an
Erinys developed from the angry soul of a dead
man, one can readily understand that she
punished the adultery of a wife with the same

severity as murder.   The Electra of Sophocles
utters this prayer :

> And ye, Erinyes, daughters of the gods,
>   Ye dreaded ones who look
> On all who perish, slain unrighteously,
> On all whose bed is stealthily defiled,
> Come ye, and help, avenge my father's death.
>
> [*Electra*, 112-116 : tr. PLUMPTRE.]

The adultery of a husband, as an offence to the
womanly feelings of his wife, was likewise condemned by custom and, in case the injured wife
made complaint, by law, but for the reasons
stated above it was not a religious transgression.

  ' A man must cling to the eternal life of the
world by leaving behind him his children's
children so that they may minister to god in
his place ', says Plato (*Laws*, 773 E), and Farnell
justly calls these words ' the most exalted conception concerning the duty of marriage and
paternity that has ever been embodied in ethical
or religious literature ' (*The Higher Aspects of
Greek Religion*, p. 36).   From this point of view
one can understand that, according to the Greek
conception, marriage was a *sacrament*.   It was
even directly called such—*telos* ;   its patrons,
the first married pair, Zeus and Hera, when their
character as such was emphasized, were called
teleioi.   To be sure, one might interpret this
epithet in a different fashion ;   but in the present
case the decisive argument is the fact that in
Athens at the marriage ceremony a boy, the son

of living parents, carried a basket of bread around the newly wedded pair, repeating meanwhile the sacramental words that the mysteries had made well known : ' I have fled from evil, I have found good '. Evil is temporality, good is eternity, both in marriage and in the mysteries : the immortality of the species, which is dependent on marriage, answers to the immortality of the soul, of which the mysteries give evidence. In complete agreement with this is the fact that the newly married pair were met in their marriage chamber by the priestess of Demeter, the goddess of the reviving grain, the goddess of the mysteries, and that only after her blessing did the marriage night begin for them. And Farnell is again perfectly correct when he says : ' St. Paul's words in his Epistle to the Ephesians (v. 32), " Great is this mystery ", which were momentous for the marriage-theory of the later Church, were in accordance both in spirit and in verbal form with earlier Hellenic religious custom rather than with Hebraic ' (*Ibid.* p. 34).

I have just called Zeus and Hera the first married pair ; in truth their ' holy marriage ' (*hieros gamos*) was the primal type of human marriages, and furthermore, as is proved by a recently discovered fragment of the oldest prose work of the Greeks, the mystical book of Pherecydes of Syros, in the minutest details of their ritual. The memory of this holy marriage was celebrated in January, which was called ' the month of marriages ' (*Gamēliōn*), in accord with the custom in agricultural Greece of contracting marriages primarily in winter. Thus the first fruits of mankind ripened at more or less the same time as the fruits of Mother Earth, and in the month Pyanepsion (October) men could celebrate both the festival of the fathers, Apaturia, and that of the mothers, Thesmophoria : a beautiful piece of evidence, in my opinion, of the eternal unity of man and nature.

This unity expressed itself still more cogently in the person of the goddess to whom women in childbed addressed their prayers. This was not Hera or even Demeter, the goddess of marriages recognized by the state, and of family life : a woman citizen brought into the world the fruit of her womb according to the same laws as every female of the woods, and one and the same goddess guarded both. This goddess we already know ; she was Artemis.

Evidently a family consecrated by such religious grace united its members by unusually strong mutual bonds. Though the law gave the father no authority over the life and death of the children, as in Rome, yet the person of the father, and in a still higher degree that of the mother, was sacred to the children. ' An old father or mother should enjoy honour in a house no less than the images of the gods ; the curses of parents reach the ears of the gods more swiftly than any others, and so it is with their

blessings ; the god himself rejoices in the honour
which children and grand-children bestow on
their parents and grand-parents ' (Plato, *Laws*,
930 E ff. abridged). And no one can set free
a son from the duty of supporting and honouring
his father to the very day of his death, provided
only that that father has not previously been
untrue to his obligations with regard to his son,
by neglecting his education. Equally holy were
the mutual obligations of brothers and sisters ;
in regard to them it is sufficient to mention the
Antigone of Sophocles. As a matter of fact,
the history of the Greek states, however many
dark pictures we may find in it, furnishes no
examples of the combat of fathers with sons or
of brothers with one another, such as so often
soil the annals of the Germanic and the Slavic
peoples. If in the fourth century Timoleon of
Corinth killed his brother, it was only because
that brother had become the tyrant of his native
land, and because in the soul of the hero, after
a fearful internal struggle, the duty of a citizen
triumphed over the duty of a brother.

But the Greek family included *slaves* as well
as freemen ; they too were united with it ' by
bonds of sprinkling ' ; they too profited by the
protection of Hestia and Zeus of the Garth.
To these deities they were presented on the day
when they were included in the family ; and
custom bade that at the same time they should
be showered with sweetmeats, as a good omen,

that they might have a ' sweet ' life in the house
of their new masters.   Progress had been made
since the Achaean epoch of Homer, seeing that
the master no longer had power over the life and
death of his menials : the murder of a slave by
his master was not only punished by the law, but
constituted a religious transgression which defiled
the house in which it was committed.   And the
Greeks were fully conscious that such a view
of the sacredness of a slave's life distinguished
them from other nations.   In general, we must
remember that the popular idea of the horrors
of ' ancient ' slavery applies only to the epoch of
the Roman *latifundia*, when the ' plantation '
system of agriculture on large tracts of land,
which had been invented by Carthage, began
to prevail.   In Greece, as Plato and the comic
writers prove, the life of slaves was quite toler-
able : their share in the common life of the
family gave their personal life far more content
than if they had been strictly confined to its
narrow bounds.   Evidently slavery must come
to an end, and it did so thanks to watchwords
first uttered by Greece itself ; but if the forms
of life are to be appraised according to the
degree of the sense of happiness native to them,
then an impartial judge will be bound to admit
that, in the final analysis, Greek society, even
the enslaved portion of it, was happier than our
own with its centrifugal tendencies, which have
long divided us from Mother Earth, which

to-day divide us from one another, and which
introduce isolation and coldness where once
there was shelter and warmth in the beams of
Hestia.

The intermediate links between the family and
the community of citizens (*polis*) were the clan,
the phratry, and the tribe (by descent). Politically they had lost their importance all over
Greece, in some places earlier, in others later—in
Athens at the time of the reforms of Clisthenes
in the year 507 B.C.—and they would have
vanished for ever, had not religion duly consecrated them, as the expanding concentric circles
of human society. So they retained religious
importance.

To be sure, the importance of the *clan* was
limited to the private cult. The clan included
families the kinship of which was proved by a
common genealogy ; Zeus was the patron of it,
but instead of Zeus *Herkeios*, as in the family,
Zeus *Homognios*, whose title expressed the
' unity of the clan '. Custom bade a man invite his kindred to family solemnities, such as
weddings, the occasions when names were given
to children, and funeral banquets. Further than
this the institution apparently amounted to
nothing.

Of greater importance was the *phratry*, which
united together clans that were derived from a
common (mythical) founder, without settled

genealogy. They had their public festival ; it was the three-day ' festival of the fathers ', with which we are already familiar, the Apaturia, in October.

The members of a phratry gathered together ; to them the happy fathers presented their new-born children along with witnesses who testi-fied to the legitimacy of their descent ; and the children were entered in the lists of members of the phratry, which, like our church records, had legal authority. This official business of course did not occupy three days : custom required a banquet, for which these same fathers provided the sacrificial beasts—a larger one (*koureion*) for a boy, and a smaller one (*meion*) for a girl. Nor was this all : the members of the phratry were also interested in the fruits of previous years, whom they had entered on the list of citizens. Boys came forward and displayed the results of their education, reciting Homer from memory —and the most eminent among the young rhapsodists received prizes.

Finally, there were festivals of the *tribes* (by descent), but we know almost nothing about them.

From the individual through the family, the clan, the phratry, and the tribe to the state was one series of steps, notably shortened during the historic epoch owing to the disappearance of three of the intermediate stages. But there was another series, which arose at the opening of the historic epoch : competing with the family organization, it gathered together similar individuals in groups, or in corporations, and in these forms of collective life subordinated them to the community of citizens. In some states the organization by groups gained the supremacy, so far as this was possible, over that by families : thus it was in Sparta. In others, of which we hear little, the family organization remained untouched. In Athens the two were of equal importance.

The *corporations*, in so far as they had a craft character, were united by a common cult of the gods who were patrons of their crafts : with these gods we are already partially acquainted. But if they were formed by voluntary association, then each of them chose its own god or guardian hero. An important part of the life of these corporations naturally consisted in observing the festivals of these gods and heroes, along with the usual sacrifices and banquets, and sometimes with games and the like. The corporations of intellectual workers, founded by poets, artists, or philosophers, are of special interest to us. After death the founder of one of them became a sort of hero for the members of the corporation who remained alive, down to late generations.

From these corporations, which united men of mature years, and often for all their lives, we distinguish the *groups* of persons of the same age, for the most part youths and maidens. Formed by the Delphic religion, they were consecrated to the Delphic deities, those of the youths to Apollo, and those of the maidens to Artemis. But this was the later Artemis, the maiden sister of Apollo, identified only by a process of historic evolution with the ancient goddess of the forest and its fertility, with whom a maiden would again come in contact when, after passing through the test of Hera and Demeter, she invoked her as the goddess of childbirth. We here touch an infinitely charming field of Greek life, the contests of youths and maidens in dance and in song. On this foundation friendship likewise developed, the cult of which was nowhere so powerful and so holy as among the Greeks. We cannot linger long upon it, although it involves an important part of Greek beauty—and Plato with his idealistic philosophy can be completely understood only on this foundation.

The crown of human society was, however, according to Greek conceptions to a greater degree than according to any others, the *state* ; or, to speak more exactly, the Hellenic variant of it, the city-state, the independent and self-sufficing *polis*. This too was naturally placed under the protection of religion—and with such zeal, with such ardour, that many modern investigators have erroneously thought it possible to consider all Greek religion from the point of view of its state character.

A myth—like all other myths, of no binding character—relates that once the gods, gathered at Sicyon (but why there in particular, we do not know), divided among themselves the cities of men. Thus Hera received Argos, the Dioscuri Sparta, Ares Thebes ; as to Athens, there was a dispute between Posidon and Pallas, which was settled in a way that we already know (p. 49). Henceforward Pallas was the goddess-guardian of Athens ; to her prayers before the throne of Zeus the city owed its life and health. When the Persian host pressed on from the East, then it seemed that

Pallas has not been able to soften the lord of Olympus,
Though she has often prayed him, and urged him with
　　excellent counsel.

And yet she succeeded in winning one boon from him :

Then far-seeing Zeus grants this to the prayers of Athene :
Safe shall the wooden wall continue for thee and thy
　　children.
　　　　　　　　　　　　[Delphic oracle, HERODOTUS, vii. 141 :
　　　　　　　　　　　　　　　　　tr. RAWLINSON.]

And thanks to the fact that the best citizen of Athens, Themistocles, succeeded in understanding correctly the will of the goddess, that the 'wooden wall ' signified the bulwarks of the vessels, her city was preserved even on this occasion.

So in Athens Pallas was the goddess ' of the

Citadel ', (*Polias, Poliouchos*) ; her festival, the
Panathenaea, which we already know and which
occurred in July, was the festival of the community as such. Many days were consecrated
to contests of all sorts, which gave the community
an opportunity to take delight in the strength,
the agility, and the beauty of its young people.
Whoever, while executing a ' dance in full
armour ', held his shield unskilfully, with a
feeble hand, lower than his breast, the citizens
put to shame, saying that he ' forgot Trito-
geneia ' (that is, Pallas). But most solemn of
all was the last day, the day of the hecatomb,
when to the goddess on her Acropolis was
presented her whole community in most beautiful and most fitting pomp, when took place the
famous ' Panathenaic procession ' to her temple
—the procession that was sculptured by Phidias
on the frieze of the Parthenon ' cella '. In it
were venerable old men with branches of the
olive, the tree of Pallas, and men in the prime of
life, with the sacrificial animals, and youths on
horseback, and the ornament of the procession,
beautiful maidens carrying baskets, and even
little girls, the ' Arrhephoroe ' ; but the heroines
of the solemn occasion were the matrons, pupils
of the goddess, who had woven in her honour the
festival peplos with a representation of her own
heroic deeds in combat with the dark powers of
the Giants, and also with the likenesses of the
most deserving citizens, whom the city by their

hands, skilled in the weaver's art, recommended to the grace of its magnanimous patroness.

The state character of Greek religion was expressed also in the fact that the *festivals of the other gods as well* were celebrated with the co-operation of the state ; this was inevitable, seeing that they must take place under the open sky, on the streets and squares, and not in the seclusion of private houses.   Nor was this all : since agonistics and, above all, choreia were an almost obligatory part of these festivals, they became a genuine school for the education of the citizens—and the democracy rightly took pains that even the poorest among them should share in their benefits.   This occasioned the intro-duction of the so-called *theorikon*, that is, the distribution of very modest doles (two or three obols apiece) to the indigent, that they might share in the solemnities.   On the other hand, these solemnities were, one may say, the greatest adornment of the life of an Athenian ; while the reveries of a modern man fly away to egoistic, centrifugal aims, in the centripetal soul of the Greek, and above all of the Athenian, they clustered about his beloved festivals, those in which all citizens participated.

To a certain degree also the *private religious feeling* of the citizens was a matter of care for the state, but only in so far as it affected the preservation of ceremonies ordained by the fathers according to the directions of the gods ;

the state did not interfere in matters of conscience. Athenian parents gladly conducted to
the temple of Athena their betrothed daughters,
and in return, after the marriage, her priestess
visited the young matron, bringing to the
woman citizen and future mother of citizens
the blessing of the goddess guardian. And when
a citizen was entrusted with a public office,
his entrance on it was preceded by an inquiry
whether he was fulfilling the obligations of his
hereditary cult, whether he was honouring the
graves of his ancestors. This inquiry was
occasioned by the fear that in case of his negli-
gence the wrath of the gods might make itself
felt even in his conduct of the public function
that had been entrusted to him.

Many men, it is true, are disturbed by certain
events which indicate that the Greeks, and in
particular the Athenians, were not entirely free
from religious intolerance. The most famous
of these is, of course, the condemnation of Socrates
by the restored Athenian democracy in the year
399 B.C. ; he was charged as follows : ' Socrates
is a doer of evil, and corrupter of the youth, and
he does not believe in the gods of the state, and
has other new divinities of his own ' (Plato,
Apology, 24 : tr. Jowett). Yet such men show
that they do not understand the case. Neither
in Athens nor anywhere else in Greece was there
a law that could be made to cover the offence
of which Socrates was accused. This is the

distinction in principle between the attitude of
Athens and of Greece towards religion and the
legalized intolerance of modern states.   According to our ideas, under such conditions no trial
can even be held, for *nullum crimen sine lege.*
In Athens this was still possible, but in this case
the blame for a show of intolerance falls not on
the state, as a permanent law-abiding institution, but on the composition of the jury in the
given case.   We know that its members acted
under the influence of the mood of the moment :
the state had just freed itself from the rule of
the ' thirty tyrants ' whose leader was Critias,
unfortunately a pupil of Socrates and apparently
an eloquent example of the ' corruption of youth'
by the seventy-year-old sage.

The Greeks can more justly be reproached
with quite the opposite quality, with excessive
tolerance for a low type of religious observances
found among foreign nations, which had free
entry into this most hospitable of lands.   To be
sure, immoral cults, with which a cruel or a
licentious ritual was blended, were forbidden.
Yet exceptions occur ;   and we must condemn
the Corinthians in that, when they were masters
of international trade in the seventh and sixth
centuries before Christ, they admitted into their
maritime city, under the name of Aphrodite, the
Semitic Astarte with her *hierodoulia,* or religious prostitution.   ' We were the rivals of the
Phoenicians,' the Corinthians would reply in

their own defence; 'we overcame them : yet
we could not refuse worship to a goddess who so
evidently was their protectress on the sea.' It
was an impious act, however, to introduce into
their own land a repulsive barbarian custom and
to defile with it the pure figure of the ancient
Hellenic goddess of love and beauty. The
Athenians, the successful rivals of the Corinthians
in the sixth and fifth centuries before Christ, did
not imitate them in this respect, and of course
they were right in not doing so.

We shall touch briefly on some other signs of
the religious consecration of civil society. Since
the state was only a further stage in the development of the family, and the city in that of the
house, we shall not be surprised at finding in the
city-state a sacred hearth as its centre, and
Hestia as the goddess of it. It was located in
the prytaneum, the meeting-place of those
organs in the state government of which the
activity never ceased ; here burned the undying
fire of the goddess, and the term *hestiouchos
polis*, ' the hearth-possessing city-state ', points
to its sanctity. As the house, beside Hestia,
possessed a representative of the male element
in its household life in the person of Zeus of the
Garth, so the state worshipped its own Zeus of
the City, *Zeus Polieus*. With his festival (the
Dipolia) was connected the ceremony of the
Bouphonia, which we have mentioned above
(p. 45) ; this fact alone is enough to prove the

ancient origin of the festival.   And Plato, as an
Athenian, was quite right when in his *Laws*
(745 B) he dedicated the Acropolis of his ideal
city to Zeus, Hestia, and Athena.

As the household worshipped the souls of
its ancestors, so the state bestowed religious
worship on the souls of its *dead citizens* at the
festival of the *Anthesteria*, which corresponded to
our All Souls' Day.   Only All Souls' Day falls
on November 2, at the close of the church year,
while the Greek religion, true to its close connection with nature, celebrated its Anthesteria
(or ' Flower Festival ') in February, when after
the frosts of winter the pores of the earth open
and, together with the first flowers of spring, the
souls of the dead fly forth from under its covering.
But the Anthesteria, as we have already seen
(p. 48), was also a festival of Dionysus ; in truth,
by virtue of a beautiful symbolism, the return
of the souls was likened to the return of the vine,
which had been buried in autumn, to the surface
of the earth in a new, spiritualized form.   The
souls were invited into the dwellings of the living ;
there they were welcomed with food, drink, and
pageants, in order to secure their favour for the
coming year, and later they were driven back to
their subterranean abode with the words : ' Out
of the door, ye souls ! the Anthesteria is over ! '
Mickiewicz, the national poet of Poland, has
described similar ceremonies and charms in his
poem *Forefathers' Eve.*

While it worshipped all souls, the city distinguished among them certain elect souls, whom it made the subject of a special cult : these were its local *heroes*, in the religious sense of the term. Often these were really men who had once lived and who by their merits had attained ' heroization ', which corresponded to the canonization of the ancient Christian religions. In cities of recent origin such in particular were their founders, ' foundation-heroes '. But since every city was founded by some one, each of them must have its founder-hero ; if tradition had not preserved his name, it was assumed to have been identical with the name of the city : that is, it was supposed that the hero gave to the city his own name. On this basis Sparta (or Lacedaemon) worshipped its hero Lacedaemon ; Corinth, its hero Corinthus. Athens was of course an exception, for this was a city founded by a deity. Yet even here there was no lack of local heroes. One of them, enigmatic enough in our time, was the hero Academus, whose grove sheltered for nine centuries the school of Plato, owing to which fact his name still lives in all our ' academies '. Cimon introduced the cult of Theseus, the king who founded Athens, if not as a city, as the capital of Attica ; the introduction of this cult was the result of the ' transfer of the relics ' of the hero from the island of Scyros to Athens. There were also other heroes.

As a matter of course, important public occasions in which the life of the city expressed itself, assemblies of the people, trials, and the like were consecrated by religious ceremonies which corresponded to our solemn divine services in similar cases. But we cannot go into details.

The Greek idea of statehood did not extend farther than the city. Nevertheless the Greeks possessed a consciousness of their *national unity*. This was based in the first place on their language, which, despite its numerous dialects, was their common possession : for this reason the Greeks contrasted themselves with the ' barbarians', a word which was originally quite innocent and meant merely men who spoke an unintelligible tongue. But their consciousness of unity rested also on their common possession of many customs (the ' common laws of Hellas '), and, above all else on the fact that they recognized the same gods under the same names. On this basis the unification of Hellas was accomplished, so far as it was accomplished at all. Its legal form was the *amphictyony*.

Amphictyons means ' those who dwell around '. Around what ? Always around a temple. A temple required protection : it possessed, besides a building, votive offerings, often of great value, flocks and herds, and land. It could not defend itself, hence the ' dwellers round about ', the amphictyons, defended it.

This was a bond that united them. Thus the cities of Euboea defended their common temple of Artemis Amarynthia; and when the two most important of them, Chalcis and Eretria, began against each other the long 'Lelantian War', in which all Greece took part (in the seventh century B.C.), they bound themselves not to employ missile weapons, and they entered their agreement on stone in the temple of Artemis. Both sides kept the treaty: Artemis was not to be trifled with; this was not 'a scrap of paper'.

There were many such amphictyonies; but the most famous was that of Delphi, founded at the dawn of history by the tribes that were then most powerful. It was mainly owing to this amphictyony that Delphi attained its dominating position among the Greek cities, as 'the common hearth of all Hellas'; the choice of this expression shows that this Hellas was understood as an expanded community, just as the community with its hearth in the prytaneum was an expanded household. The beneficent results of this religious unification for all inter-Hellenic politics were expressed in this treaty also: 'We take an oath not to allow a city belonging to the amphictyony to be destroyed, not to deprive it of drinking water either in war or in peace, and to declare war on a state which may venture to do such a thing'. These promising beginnings unfortunately did not fully produce the fruits that might have been expected

of them ; so far as one can judge, this was due to
two causes. In the first place, of the states that
concluded the treaty, several had completely
lost their importance in the historic epoch, and
yet in the Amphictyonic Council they all enjoyed
their former right of representation along with
Athens and Sparta, in consequence of which the
Council, as a representative organ, ceased to
correspond to the political organization of Greece.
And in the second place, Delphi in the sixth and
fifth centuries, yielding to the temptations of
international politics, was untrue to its significance in Greece as the support of national ideals
against the Persians. Had it not been for these
two causes, the ' common hearth of Hellas '
would have become its great prytaneum under
the protection of Zeus of all Hellas and of his
powerful son Apollo. In this fashion the future
religion of Hellas was outlining itself.

Other centres of the religious unification of the
Greeks were their *national games*, which also had
a cult character : the games of Zeus at Nemea
and, most important, at Olympia, of Posidon at
the Isthmus, of Apollo at Delphi. Here also
belong the mysteries of Eleusis, after the date
when, by the will of the same Delphian Apollo,
they had been recognized as of importance for
all Hellas.

Of the *common laws of Hellas* mentioned above,
some, if not all, likewise had a religious sanction.
I will mention the two most important.

We already know *Hermes* and his potent wand
—the wand with serpents—the symbol of security among foreigners and enemies. In the hands
of his servants, *heralds*, it protected not only
the heralds themselves but persons who accompanied them ; and therefore in times of war
the office of herald acquired an inter-Hellenic
character. The words, ' Henceforward these
two states did not communicate with each other
except through heralds', meant that they were in
a state of war. I beg you to notice how Hermes
now grows in stature before our very eyes ;
Hermes, that ' god of thieves ', as he is con-
ceived by men who mistake playful mythology
for religion. No, all that sort of thing one should
simply forget as completely as may be. ' If
I ply this herald-craft of Hermes with any sure-
ness, I will never trip in doing thine errand ',
says the herald Lichas in Sophocles (*Trachiniae*,
620, 621 : tr. Jebb). ' If any herald or ambassador carry a false message to any other city, or
bring back a false message from the city to which
he is sent, or be proved to have brought back,
whether from friends or enemies, in his capacity
of herald or ambassador, what they have never
said, let him be indicted for having offended,
contrary to the law, in the sacred office and
appointment of Hermes and Zeus ', says Plato
(*Laws*, 941 A : tr. Jowett). Such are the voices
of genuine religion. And there was no trifling
with him : when the Argive herald Copreus fell

at Athens as a victim of popular ' lynch law ',
the divinities of Eleusis, who in that city watched
over the rights of Hermes, laid a penance upon
Athens from which the city was liberated only a
thousand years later.

The second of these laws pertained to *supplication* (*hikesia*) and *hospitality*, two kindred
institutions, which were united by the common
care of Zeus himself. A foreigner, even an
enemy, was sacred if with an olive branch in
his hand he took refuge at the altar of a god ;
Zeus Hikesios protected him and defended him
from wrong. There were, however, even simpler
ceremonies of supplication ; as a last resort it
sufficed to touch with a supplicating hand a
man's hand, knees, or chin, in order to secure for
oneself his protection in the name of Zeus.
Closely connected with this custom was the right
of *asylum*, which in some measure was associated
with all sacred places, but with certain of them
to a peculiar degree. Evidently in all cases of
this sort there was danger of abuse ; the legal
feeling of well-ordered communities could not
allow a criminal to escape deserved punishment
through supplication or asylum. But in any
case a foreigner and an enemy, as such, had safety
assured him.

A no less effective means of escape was *hospitality*, which in Greece was observed with special
sanctity : ' honour the gods ', ' honour thy
parents ', ' honour a guest ', such were the three

most important commandments for a Greek. At first only private bonds of hospitality were recognized. These, however, were hereditary : the Achaean Diomedes and Glaucus, an ally of the Trojans, lower their spears before each other and even exchange armour, concluding a sort of brotherhood, as soon as they have recognized each other as ' guest-friends of old times through their fåthers ' (*Iliad*, vi. 215 : tr. Leaf). But more frequently men recognized each other by means of the two halves of a tablet (*symbolon*), which in old times the fathers or ancestors of the men concerned had broken in half when they concluded their bond of hospitality.

But since the community was an enlarged family and possessed its own hearth, guarded by Hestia, a bond of hospitality was also possible with the community as a whole : thus arose the institution of *proxeny*, corresponding in some measure to our consulate. For example, Cimon, who was an Athenian, was the *proxenos* of Sparta at Athens : the meaning of the office was as follows. Whenever Cimon made a trip to Sparta, he was the guest of the state there ; if a Spartan came to Athens, he was the guest of Cimon and enjoyed his protection in all his affairs. Thus under the patronage of Zeus the Hospitable (*Zeus Xenios*) an inter-Hellenic law made its appearance in hospitable Hellas.

Could even an *international law* have developed

from this ?   In other words : did Greek religion
recognize humanity as well as Hellas ?   Here we
come upon a trait in it which is alone sufficient
to give it a higher position than any religion
contemporary with it : while Jehovah was still
only the tribal god of his ' chosen people ' and
recognized other nations only as the tools of his
rewards or his punishments, the Homeric Zeus
was the god of all humanity and looked with
equal kindness on the Greek and on the Greek's
foe, if the foe deserved it.

> Ah—I behold a warrior dear to me
> Around the walls of Ilium driven, and grieve—
> > [*Iliad*, xxii. 168, 169 : tr. COWPER.]

Thus he speaks of Hector, the principal foe of
the Achaeans beneath the walls of Troy.   I should
like to have the reader of this book remember
these two verses better than aught else, that
they may be the first thing to arise in his consciousness at the mention of the words ' Greek
religion '.

This came to pass because the Greek ' was not
so spellbound by the magic of the name but that
he was capable of the humane and tolerant idea
that seemed so hard for the Semitic mind of
Israel to grasp—namely, that mankind might
worship the same godhead under different
names ' (Farnell, *Ibid*. p. 106).   We find this
idea already clearly expressed in the profound
prayer of Aeschylus to Zeus :

O Zeus—whoe'er he be,
If that name please him well,
By that on him I call.

> [*Agamemnon*, ed. Weil, 160-162 : tr.
> adapted from PLUMPTRE.]

' The cruellest fanaticism and the most savage
religious wars have been stimulated partly by
this fallacious sentiment concerning the magic
of names. The Greek escaped all this, nor did any
religious war in the true sense of the word stain
the pages of Greek history ; and no unhappy
logic compelled him to degrade the deities of
other peoples into the rank of devils. If the
modern man has arrived at the conception that
difference of divine title is of little import, a
conception of priceless value for the cause of
human unity, he owes it mainly, as Rome owed
it, to the mind of Hellas ' (Farnell, *Ibid.* pp.
106, 107).

At first, when Hellenism was confined to the
boundaries of its own country, the result of this
conception was merely tolerance for the religions of other peoples. Let the reader review
the history of Herodotus from this point of view,
and he will be convinced that for the Greek
there are no 'pagans'. 'The Thracians worship
Ares ' ; ' the Egyptians worship Zeus (Ammon),
Demeter (Isis), Athena (Hator) '; ' the Persians
worship Apollo ' ; and so on. It is perfectly
clear that all humanity worships the same gods,
that all humanity forms a harmonious religious

whole. On the basis of this conception Delphi made an attempt to extend its religion to all humanity. In the West it succeeded: Rome of the Tarquins recognized Apollo and under his influence identified the Greek gods with its own, even accepting their ritual to a marked degree; henceforward we have Zeus-Jove and the like. In the East it also had some success at first, in the time of Croesus; but when Croesus, by crossing the Halys, 'destroyed a powerful kingdom '—his own—and Delphi yearned to take under its protection the victorious Persians, it lost thereby a part of its influence in Greece, and yet failed to unite the world under the ensign of the religion of god the father and god the son. For that the 'time must be fulfilled'.

On the other hand, when Alexander the Great removed the barrier between Hellenism and the barbarian East, when his successors with the aid of their Graeco-Macedonian armies became the rulers of oriental kingdoms, then the time came for their religious unification. And we must deeply regret that the sources give us such scanty information of the apostle of Demeter of Eleusis, who was the principal creator of this unification; of *Timotheus*, the hierophant of Eleusis. So much we know, that—probably in the time of Lysimachus—he accomplished the fusion of the mysteries of Eleusis with the Asiatic cult of the Great Mother of the gods in Pessinus (Cybele), whereby the religion of this

Mother became the official religion of the Kingdom of Pergamum ; we know also that this same
Timotheus under Ptolemy Soter accomplished
the fusion of the mysteries of Eleusis with the
cult of Isis in Egypt, whereby the religion of
Zeus-Sarapis and of Demeter-Isis became the
official religion of the dominions of the Ptole-
mies. Both cults were later transferred to
Greece and to Rome—to that Rome which was
already the whole world. And when this Roman
world reorganized Christianity, the two cults
with their united strength gave to the new
religion its goddess. This is not a conjecture ;
this is a documented fact. When Gregory the
Theologian, gratifying the religious needs of his
faithful Christians, permitted them to worship
the Mother of God, the fanatics among the
Christians murmured, saying : ' But this is
Isis ! '—' But this is the Great Mother ! ' They
would have been still more correct if they had
said : ' But this is Demeter, the mother of
sorrows, the comforter and consoler of the
afflicted ! '

VI

THE REVELATION OF GOD IN GOODNESS

'EVERY man should strive to keep his soul pure
and free from evil of every sort, for the gods
accept no worship from evil men. They are not
served by rich gifts and magnificent offerings,
but by virtue and a will directed towards justice
and goodness. Therefore every man who wishes
to be dear to the gods should be good to the
extent of his power, both in act and will. . . .
He should remember that the gods exist and that
they punish the unjust ; and he should always
have in mind the time when he must depart from
life. For all men when about to die repent,
remembering their unjust acts, and bitterly
yearn that they might always have acted
justly. . . . And if an evil demon stands beside
him, urging him to injustice, then he should seek
shelter in the temples, at the altars and in the
holy places, fleeing from injustice as a most
unholy and grievous mistress, and supplicating
the gods to aid him in driving her from him'
(Stobaeus, ed. Hense, vol. iv. pp. 124, 125).

These notable words occurred in the introduction to the code of Zaleucus, the oldest written legislation of Greece. To be sure, somebody else wrote them. Zaleucus lived in the seventh century before Christ, in Locri in Italy ; but his code at various dates, and with appropriate alterations, passed to other Grecian states, and during one of these transfers our introduction may have been added. At any rate it belongs to the epoch of which we are speaking. In it, in a clear form, the conviction became crystallized which, with a diffused light, illumines the rest of the literature of that epoch, the conviction that the Greek religion was a religion in the highest degree ethical, that the Greek god revealed himself in goodness.

It was not always so. Primitively both in Greece and everywhere else god revealed himself not in justice, but in power, and the *Homeric* epoch was an epoch of the gradual fusion of 'god' and 'good' into one concept. And undoubtedly, if Greece, like Israel, had lived under the rule of a powerful priesthood, that priesthood would have carefully obliterated every trace of a primitive pre-moral conception of the deity. Happily this was not the case— the orderly sequence of various layers in the Homeric poems makes it possible for us to observe more or less exactly the curious and important process of the gradual moralization of the Greek religion. At first the god watches exclusively, but extremely jealously, over man's strictly religious duty, that is, his fulfilment of his obligations towards him, the god ; later he extends his care to those human relations which, owing to the weakness of one of the parties, may easily tempt the other to abuse his power : such are the relations of sons to their grey-haired parents and of a householder to an un-armed guest. Finally, the entire moral duty of man becomes the object of the divine *opis*—to use the name given by Homer in the *Odyssey* to the all-seeing punitive power of the divinity.

After the Homeric epoch came the epoch marked by the prevailing influence of the Delphic *Apollo*. To it we owe definite progress in the field which we are discussing, mingled at first, to be sure, with certain deviations from the straight path marked out by the evolution of the Homeric epoch. Owing to the primitive significance of Apollo as god of the sun, the pos-tulate of *purity* (*hagneia*) became the principal postulate of the religion of Apollo. Hateful to the god is all that defiles man and through man the god himself—all *pollution* (*miasma*) ; the pollution of pollutions was murder ; next came adultery, and so on. In this book I cannot sketch the history of the development of the concept of pollution : I take it in its final form.

The danger of the deviation mentioned above depended on the fact that pollution could be understood independently of intention, as ' self-sufficing pollution '; the shedding of all human blood defiles, even if it be shed involuntarily or in just self-defence ; and the most criminal plan does not defile, if, in consequence of circumstances independent of the planner, it fails to succeed. All contact with a murderer defiles, all conversation with him, and the like, for pollution acts like contagion. Another danger was inherent in the broadening of the concept : the shedding of all blood defiles, even if it be that of a beast ; so do all sexual relations, even in marriage. Great was the temptation of (religious) vegetarianism and that of the worship of an antiphysical virginity ; and indeed here and there we meet with the realization of them : of the first in Pythagoreanism, of the second in a movement of which we find evidence in the *Hippolytus* of Euripides. Finally, since of course Apollo himself was the god who purified one from pollution, and since purification took place by means of religious rites, therefore there was also great danger of *ritualism* ; that is, that the rites of purification would be recognized as self-sufficing, independently of the mental attitude of the person subject to them : in other words, to appeal to a medieval analogy, that in the religion of Apollo there would prevail not the point of view of St. Thomas Aquinas, but that of Duns Scotus, and that religious justification would be recognized as possible *ex opere operato sine bono motu auctoris*, from the act performed without any good intention on the part of the doer.

In the development of the religion of Apollo the seventh and the sixth centuries were an epoch of struggle, which to some degree continued even in the fifth century ; this struggle ended with the victory of the moral principle. A main cause of this victory was the Pythagorean school of prophets ; upholding vegetarianism (principally from eschatological views, of which we shall speak later), it nevertheless contended energetically and successfully with an external understanding of purity, with self-sufficing pollution and with ritualism. I may cite as an illustration the reply of the prophetess Theano— I must, however, first forewarn the reader that the Greek word *anēr*, like the German *Mann*, signifies both *man* and *husband*—so when she was presented with the query, an important one for the religious life of woman in the family, how soon ' after the man ' a woman becomes clean, the prophetess replied : ' After her own at once, after another never' (Stobaeus, ed. Hense, iv. 586).

In the Greek tragedy of the fifth century we still perceive traces of the old theory of self-sufficing pollution and of ritualism ; in the fourth century the moral point of view conquered. Purifying rites were recognized as having a certain importance, which after all rightly belongs to them, as a powerful means of acting on the feelings and the frame of mind of the believer; but purity of soul was given the first place. This point of view is very beautifully expressed by the epigram of the Delphic priestess:

Pure be thy soul when thou ent'rest the most pure temple of godhead ;
First let the Castalian spring wash all stain from thy limbs.
Good men need but a drop, O pilgrim. But if thou art wicked,
Then the waves of the sea never will banish thy stain.

Returning to the gains by the Homeric epoch, we shall easily detect still another danger, which, however, many men do not regard as a danger at all. God stands on guard over moral obligation in its full extent and punishes offenders against it : should we then be moral in order to avoid punishment ? Because of terror ?

Of course in the last analysis even this is good —and nobody will deny that the *fear of God* is a powerful moral stimulus. The religious morality of the Homeric epoch created this very term ; it terms godfearing (*theoudēs*) a man or a people that, for example, behaves kindly towards foreigners. It is easy to understand the matter : the gods dwell on high in the heavens and man sees them not ; but when the autumn rains deluge his fields and destroy the grain that he has planted, then he knows that Zeus is inflicting punishment for unjust sentences passed in the market-place. So he fears Zeus.

But then came the times of the religion of
Apollo ; the gods began to dwell among men, in
beautiful temples, themselves beautiful and
gracious, in so far as artists succeeded in repro-
ducing their forms in the images that they
fashioned ; the civil calendar began to glow with
the colours of beautiful festivals, celebrated with
ever more enchanting ceremonies, which gradually changed the Greek religion into a religion of
joy—in the face of this sea of beauty the former
terror could not endure.   One must fear the
Erinyes : so men strove not to mention their
name, and passed by the gloomy grotto dedicated to them beneath the crag of the Acropolis
only with gentle steps and with a gentle prayer.
In general, the word 'godfearing' (in its new
form *deisidaimōn*) began to mean superstitious ;
a man of normal faith did not fear his gods but
loved them.

In very truth, now for the first time there
came into general use an epithet which the
Homeric Greek had not yet ventured to bestow
upon his gods, the epithet 'dear'.   In Homeric
times men did no more than recognize that a
god could love a mortal.   'Love me to-day,
O Athena,' Diomedes prays before a desperate
combat (compare p. 136, below), and ' the Muse
loved more than other men ' the bard Demodo-
cus (*Odyssey*, viii. 62).   But still man had not
yet ventured to reply to that love with a return
of affection : terror does not permit the rise of

a gentler feeling.   Now the barrier was removed.
' Dear Zeus ', ' dear Apollo ', ' dear Artemis ',
we hear at every step, so frequently that we do
not even notice the word.   A festival is observed
that the hearts of the gods may rejoice ; and
even a modest song, sung at table in honour of a
god, has as its favourite ending : ' Smile upon
my song, O god ! '   So when we hear that a man
always consecrates to a god objects which,
though they have no inherent worth, have
become significant to him at a time when with
peculiar clearness he has felt over him the saving
arm of a god who loves him—thus a shipwrecked
man dedicates to Posidon his wet clothing,
obviously far from costly ;   a prisoner, whom
the love of a pirate's daughter has preserved
from death, consecrates his chains to Aphrodite ;
and even women in childbed offer their tunics
to Artemis—is it not plain that the same love
is at work which among men in similar circumstances gives worth to even the least valuable
objects ?

And as for children who love their parents
there is no more bitter punishment than separa-
tion from them, so for a Greek it was a most
grievous feeling that, owing to his sins, the gods
would not allow him to approach their presence,
that he would be forbidden to enter the holy
Acropolis, that he would not behold Pallas,
goddess of his fathers, that he would not share
with others the soul-exalting ceremonies of the

public festivals, that he would even be excluded
from a sacrifice in the quiet of his home, with its
prayer and sprinkling.

Now let me inquire : Where again shall we
find a similar foundation for religious ethics,
a similar relation of man to God ?—In Christianity ? Yes, most assuredly. A Pole's most
frequent formula of asseveration is, ' As I love
God ', and the words *lieber Gott* have become the
most usual epithet used by a German. Yet it
may not be superfluous to put the question :
Which of the two rivers that united in Christianity brought with it that joyous feeling ?

When in the Graeco-Roman world there arose
the first societies of people who worshipped the
God of Israel, they distinguished themselves from
others and were themselves distinguished by
others by an official title, ' Men who fear God '
(*phoboumenoi ton theon*).

And when the Stoics finished building the
structure of autonomic ethics begun by Plato,
they needed only to put in place of the divinity
their own goddess, virtue, in order to obtain
the same distinction between the free soul and
the slavish soul :

'Tis love of right that keeps the good from wrong ;
You do no harm because you fear the thong.
[Horace, *Epistles*, i. 16. 52, 53 : tr. Conington.]

The ethical character attained by the religion
of ancient Greece in its flourishing epoch is also

expressed in the customary methods of worship, which, without reference to the individual features of each festival, are common to all of them, and also to the private cult in its manifold manifestations. For the most part these are gifts (and more particularly *sacrifices*) offered to the gods, and *prayers*.

By sacrifices I mean all varieties of them, from the modest incense or libation to which men constantly resorted, thus mingling with every moment of life that was important in itself the warmth of a symbolic communion with the deity, up to the solemn hecatomb. Here religio-ethical progress depended on the fact that the centre of gravity was constantly shifted from the material worth of the sacrifice to the devout temper of the man offering it. Beginnings of the process already existed in very ancient times : as has been said above, among the Greeks even a sacrifice by fire was not a holocaust, but a banquet shared by gods and men, while into the fire were cast those parts of the beast that had small value as food. If the rough-hewn peasant intellect of Hesiod could interpret this custom only by the supposition that Zeus—voluntarily, to be sure—let himself be deceived by Prometheus, the friend of humanity, he himself is responsible for such an explanation, while it is a fact that even in Homeric times true believers understood that the rite which they performed had symbolic

and not material value. Under these conditions
the hecatombs, both public and private, furnished
a generous meal for the poor, to whom they
offered the only opportunity for regaling themselves on meat. So the plenteousness of them
was dear to the god as an act of kindness in his
name. Must we then conclude that a rich man
possessed more ample means of winning the
favour of the gods than a poor man ? Such was
the opinion of many men in the fifth century—
and the venerable old man Cephalus in Plato's
Republic (331 B), when asked what he regards
as the best feature of his wealth, replies in that
spirit : ' That I depart to the other world without
fear, being a debtor neither to the gods nor to
men.'

Yet the best minds of Greece struggled with
this danger of the materialization of the sacrifice
—and struggled successfully. The result of that
struggle is expressed for example in the words
ascribed to Zaleucus that have been cited above ;
as time went on the worth of the ' widow's mite '
was more and more recognized. To it Horace,
the propagator of Hellenic ideas among the
Romans, dedicated one of his most beautiful
odes, full of the deepest feeling (*Odes*, iii. 23).

What I have said of sacrifices, as banquets
shared by gods and men, pertains to only one
class of them—the most frequent, to be sure—
the sacrifices of supplication. There were,
however, sacrifices of other sorts, of which I shall

mention only one class, the most grave and awful, the *sacrifices of expiation*. They are connected, not with a joyous and confident, but with an oppressed attitude on the part of the sacrificers —oppressed by the undoubted wrath of the god, which no prayers can appease. In such cases men sometimes had recourse to an ancient symbolic rite ; they selected a beast which was to be the ' scapegoat ', bade it bear the sin and the pollution of the whole people, and conse-crated it to the wrathful gods, sometimes by burning it entire (*holokauston*), sometimes by burying it or casting it into the sea. This is a remarkable idea, which passed into the most mysterious sacrament of the Christian religion— *Agnus Dei qui tollit peccata mundi*, ' The Lamb of God that taketh away the sins of the world '. And from the idea in both cases there develops a terrible rite—' It is expedient for you that one man should die for the people, and that the whole nation perish not ' (John xi. 50)—the rite of an expiatory *human sacrifice*.

It was universal both in the east and in the west, in the north and in the south ; once on a time even Hellas practised it—we are all familiar with the sacrifice of Iphigenia ; and the beauti-ful legend of Jephthah's daughter has an almost exact parallel in the Greek legend of Idomeneus, King of Crete, who also once thoughtlessly vowed that he would offer in sacrifice to the gods whatever should come forth to meet him—

and unexpectedly he met his own son. But
the Cretans banished Idomeneus owing to his
godless sacrifice ; and Artemis did not accept
the blood of Iphigenia from Agamemnon, but at
the critical moment substituted for her a doe.

In the historical epoch the healthy feeling of
Greece contends victoriously with this terrible
survival.   Here a man is replaced by a sacrificial
animal, disguised as a man ; there, by a doll.
Here the man remains a man, but his sacrifice is
replaced by the sprinkling of the altar with his
blood, or else he is thrown from a crag, after due
care has been taken that he escape without
injury.   Finally, in other places, and very
rarely—and this was the most scrupulous attitude towards ancient traditions—a criminal
condemned to death was designated as a sacrifice.
In each case we have to deal with so-called
pharmakoi, or means of ' healing ' the land
from illness.   And in all these transformations,
not excluding the last, there is expressed a
consciousness that a human sacrifice cannot be
reconciled with the religio-moral feeling of
historic Greece.   From this same point of view
Euripides protests against the horrible ritual of
the barbaric Artemis of the Taurians :

Rather I suspect that the natives of this land, being
cannibals themselves, impute this failing to their deity ;
for I cannot believe that any god is such a sinner.

[*Iphigenia among the Taurians*, 389-391 :
tr. COLERIDGE.]

Turning to *prayer*, we can observe here also the same progress in a moral direction. A Greek prayer is usually composed of three parts : the invocation, the entreaty, and the sanction. Let us take as an example one of the oldest and the most beautiful, the prayer to Apollo of his priest Chryses, whose daughter the Achaeans have given to Agamemnon as a paramour :

> God of the silver bow, who with thy power
> Encirclest Chryse, and who reign'st supreme
> In Tenedos and Cilla the divine,
> Sminthian Apollo !

This is the invocation (*theologia*) : the man praying heaps up epithets, judging that it is pleasant to the god to hear of his own power and dignities, and not wishing, so far as he is able, to omit a single one of the sides of the activity of the god whom he is invoking.

> If I e'er adorned
> Thy beauteous fane, or on thy altar burned
> The fat acceptable of bulls or goats—

This is the *sanction :* the man praying appeals to the services which he himself has rendered to the god, in order that he may thereby incline him to hearken to his prayer.

> Grant my petition.   With thy shafts avenge
> On the Achaean host thy servant's tears.
>   [*Iliad*, i. 37-42 : tr. Cowper.]

This is the *entreaty* (*euchē*)—in the present case an entreaty for vengeance, for punishment :

in substance the prayer amounts to a curse.
' And Apollo heard the prayer.'

In all three parts of the prayer progress was
possible and was attained.

The noisy verbosity of the *invocation* was at
bottom innocent, and therefore was long preserved ; and yet we feel the growth of an ethical
power in the invocation by Aeschylus that has
already been mentioned :

> O Zeus—whoe'er he be,
> If that name please him well,
> By that on him I call.

[See pp. 77, 119.]

More important was the *sanction*. In the
prayer of Chryses, despite all its beauty, it
nevertheless amounts to pointing out to the
god his duty. Yes, his duty ; and therefore
the later prayer of Diomedes to Pallas, which
I have also already mentioned (p. 128), stands
higher from a moral point of view : the hero
does not appeal to his own merits, but, on the
contrary, to the *love* which the goddess has
already frequently shown him :

> Unconquered daughter of Zeus, Aegis-armed !
> If ever me, propitious, or my sire
> Thou hast in furious fight helped heretofore,
> Now show thy love for me.

[*Iliad*, v. 115-117 : tr. adapted from COWPER.]

And on the same basis rests the prayer of
Sappho to Aphrodite, one of the most heartfelt
and the most moving that have been preserved

to us. We have before us a loving woman, whose affection has been spurned by her beloved. . . .

May a Christian woman in prayer give free expression to feelings of the same earthly sort ? I think that the Mother of God accepts even such prayers, if they are sincere and if the feeling of injury that has called them forth is likewise sincere. But at all events Aphrodite accepted them :

> Come in thy pity—come, if I have prayed thee ;
> Come at the cry of my sorrow : in the old times
> Oft thou hast heard, and left thy father's heaven,
>   Left the gold houses.
>   [Tr. Edwin Arnold.]

Once on a time men were certainly familiar with still another sanction : man appealed to his own power over the divinity, which he had gained by magic means ; he did not ask, but demanded and threatened ; the prayer was a *conjuration*. Such was at all times the attitude of the Egyptians to their gods ; but for the Greek this is a hypothetical oldest epoch of superstition, of which even in the Homeric epoch, not to speak of the historical, there remained no trace whatever—if we leave out of account certain low fields of private magic.

Finally—the *entreaty*.—For what is it proper to ask ? Obviously the desire for retribution is a natural feeling, especially if great wrong has been done to some one ; and Plato himself admits

that the curse of a father or mother, to whom
his children have done wrong, will infallibly
reach the ears of the gods.   From this point of
view one can also understand that even the State,
the common mother of all citizens, at times
invokes the punishment of the gods against her
evil sons who by flight have escaped the punishment of public justice.   And yet—what nobility
breathes from the reply of Theano, the priestess
of Demeter !   When the Athenian democracy,
enraged at the treachery of Alcibiades, addressed
all the priests and priestesses with a demand
that they cast on him a curse in the name of
their gods, she alone did not comply with the
demand, but replied: 'I am the priestess of
prayers and not of curses ' (Plutarch, *Alcibiades*).

God is goodness and only good proceeds from
him, taught Plato ; and therefore it is proper to
ask him only for what is good.   Great was the
temptation to understand this good in a low
sense and to address the gods with such prayers
as, in the ironic phrase of the later Stoic Persius,
could be communicated to them only if one
took them aside.   In order to counteract this
low conception, old Pythagoras had already
demanded that every prayer should be spoken
aloud.   The states in their official prayers set
a good example in this respect : Athens prayed
' for the good and the unity of Athenian citizens,
their wives and children, and the whole country ;
and likewise for those of the allies ' ; Sparta,

that the gods should give her ' beauty along with
the good '. But highest of all, obviously, was
the prayer which Plato, or his school, puts into
the mouth of Socrates : ' Lord Zeus, grant us
good even without our request ; grant us not
evil, even at our request ' (*Alcibiades II.* 143A).

Yet one may ask whether such a conception
of prayer be not a negation of it. ' No,'
answered Neoplatonism, ' for prayer exalts the
soul to immediate communion with the deity.'
(Compare Proclus, *In Timaeum*, 64A.) In this
way was attained the highest point in the religio-
moral conception of prayer.

Hitherto we have been speaking of religion for
good men ; but the nation contains also evil
men, and many of them too. Then let the
thought of *divine punishment* restrain them from
crime, if they have no feeling for communion
in love.

Of divine punishment, but where ? In this
world or in the next ? Zaleucus speaks of both ;
we too shall speak of both.

God in this world rewards the good and
punishes the evil. What does that mean ? It
means that the prosperity of the good and the
misfortunes of the evil, independently of the
natural causes that have produced them, are
understood as the reward or punishment sent by
the deity. For all acts and experiences of man
are connected with one another by a double

causality, natural and supernatural, and these causalities do not mutually exclude each other, but exist side by side : such is the ' law of double vision ' which I have established, something analogous to the ' psycho-physical parallelism ' recognized by some modern philosophers.

Excellent : so long as the good man is happy and the bad man unhappy, all is in order. Yet the reverse occurs—experience is inexorable— and frequently at that. Where then is the divine *opis*, or, as later men will say, divine *providence* (*pronoia*, Latin *providentia*) ? Herein there is a barrier, but it is not hard to overcome it. Triumph not, O criminal ; lose not hope, O just man ; await what will occur later : ' The mills of the gods grind slowly, but they grind exceeding small.'

Very good, we will wait. . . .   And now we have waited, until death. The criminal has died in prosperity, the just man in misfortune. Where are ye now, ye mills of the gods ?

This is the stumbling-block. The author of the Book of Job, even before reaching it, was cast down in spirit and found salvation from despair only in the mist of agnosticism. The Greek was happily borne over the abyss of despair by faith in Mother Earth and her laws. Here we come to a view important in ancient ethics, in distinction from modern ethics, which I have called *phylonomism*, contrasting it to the *ontonomism* of the present day—the terms are selected by analogy with the *phylogenesis* and *ontogenesis* of Haeckel.

So we have waited until death—and we have paused, thinking that it is—I repeat, in this world —the end. And here we have made a mistake ; death is not the end. Beyond or above its boundaries the life of the individual endures further—in the species.

' That is a truism.' So far it really is one ; and obviously phylonomism does not depend on this statement. It depends on the fact that the individual *is conscious* that he forms a single whole with his species in an ascending and descending line ; that he is conscious of a load of responsibility laid on him by his ancestors, and at the same time of another, which he is laying on his posterity. Phylonomism is a phenomenon of consciousness and not of natural history.

In most recent times the growth of science, with a brutality that we have merited by our apostasy, has placed us face to face with this truth that we had forgotten, and is building up before us the terrible problem of *heredity*. Yes, by our physical nature we verily gather fruits sown by our ancestors and answer for their sins—without any merit or fault on our own part. . . . Our own ? Ridiculous reservation ! Are they not ourselves ?

The Greek long ago anticipated this problem and settled it on the basis of his phylonomic

consciousness. . . .   The humblest farm servant
was then an aristocrat, compared with whom
the most royal of the kings of to-day in his
ontonomic poverty betrays himself as a plebeian.
The species not only is immortal, but feels itself
so in every individual of it.

The descendant must answer for the sins of
his ancestors—that is just as natural as the fact
that an old man must answer for the sins of his
youth.   If a man is overtaken by a misfortune
which he has not deserved by anything in his
life as an individual, his first thought is that he
is paying a penance for the sin of some one of his
ancestors :

> On mine head have I gathered the load
> Of the far-off sins of an ancient line ;
> And this is the vengeance of God !
> > [EURIPIDES, *Hippolytus*, 831-833 :
> > > tr. WAY.]

Thus exclaims the Theseus of Euripides at the
news of the sudden death of his young wife
Phaedra.   The religious ethics of the ' tragic
epoch ' of Greece personified this hereditary sin
under the name *Alastor* ; an important part of
Greek tragedy, especially in the trilogies of
Aeschylus, is built on this belief.   Whether that
conception had penetrated the deep layers of
popular belief we do not know, but that is not
the point at issue.   ' From the gods a perjurer
cannot find concealment, nor can he escape
their punishment ; and if not he himself, then

the children and all the race of the perjurer
encounter great disaster ': such are the words,
even at the end of the fourth century (compare
below, p. 181), of the spiritual leader of Athens
at that time, the magistrate and orator Lycurgus
(*Against Leocrates*, 79).

In this manner faith in divine providence was
preserved. Does the good man die in misfortune ? Let him comfort himself, contemplating
his posterity : his good deeds will shelter them
with the warm cloak of divine grace, under which
life will be good for them.—Does the evil man die
in prosperity ? Let him tremble at the thought
of Alastor, whom he has introduced into his
house by his crimes, giving it over to him to be
consumed and condemning his own posterity to
disasters and destruction.—And if both of them
are childless ? Then both of them are *already*
punished, the good man for the crimes of his
ancestors, the evil man for his own—and, moreover, their punishment is as terrible as the
punishing hand of the deity can inflict upon
them.

In very truth, one conviction lies at the basis
of ancient phylonomism and of the general
ancient view of the world : 'Children are a
blessing, childlessness is a misfortune.' Euripides gives expression to the idea : ' Ah ! yes,
his children are to every man as his own soul ;
and whoso sneers at this through inexperience,
though he suffers less anguish, yet tastes the

bitter in his cup of bliss ' (*Andromache*, 418-420 : tr. Coleridge).

Here meet the threads that proceed from ancient religion : from one side, as a religion of nature ; from the other, as a religion of society— the physical thread and the political thread. And here we note the force of the words, full of deep meaning, that accompanied the sacrament of marriage : ' I have fled from evil, I have found good ' (see p. 96, above).

In this world—that is one side of the question, for many men the principal consideration, but yet it is not the whole thing : the teachings of Zaleucus speak also of *punishment in the other world*. This need not surprise us : the Christian view is more or less the same. Yet there is a difference in the degree of certainty felt by man on these two subjects.

Curious in this respect are the words of Cephalus, the representative of the religious morality of the average Greek, whom I have mentioned above (p. 132) : 'When a man thinks himself to be near death, fears and cares enter into his mind which he never had before ; the tales of a world below and the punishment which is enacted there of deeds done here, were once a laughing matter to him, but now he is tormented with the thought that they may be true ' (Plato, *Republic*, 330 D : tr. Jowett).

As a matter of fact, there was no dogmatic

clearness on this topic ; various views coexisted, the fruits of the religious consciousness of various epochs. The soul lives after the death of the body, so much is fully recognized : but how ? It abides invisibly, as a kindly ghost, in the house of its descendants ; or it dwells near the body in the tomb, where also one should care for it, but it visits its own former house at the festival of the Anthesteria, or, along with other souls, it dwells in the common realm of all the shades, in the precincts of Hades, which are sometimes imagined as being at the western borders of the earth, beyond Oceanus, and sometimes beneath the earth. In all this there is as yet no moral element ; we are dealing with a side of ancient religion called *animism*.

Nor is there any directly moral element in a phenomenon, characteristic of Greece, on which I have already touched from time to time —in *heroization*. The hero in a formally religious sense is a glorified mortal. He possesses full consciousness (*pampsychos*) ; as transfigured, he is clad in the highest beauty (*eumorphos*) ; he is happy in his power and in the worship that he receives (*makarios*). He is united with the living by a bond of love ; his memory is honoured by them in the second of the three libations at banquets : the new Attic comedy frequently represented him as the guardian spirit of the house faithful to him, as the defender from wrong of orphans left without a guardian. But for what reason was the honour of heroization granted to a mortal ?   Not always for the moral deserts of his life.

Yet there existed a teaching which opened wide the gates of eschatology to the stream of morality ; this teaching, however, was secret, was for the initiated. I refer to the *mysteries* (from the verb *myein*, ' to close the eyes ' ; the initiate must sever himself from the external world for the purpose of internal contemplation). Of such mysteries there were several varieties in Greece ; but I shall limit myself to the two principal types, the Eleusinian mysteries of Demeter and the Orphic mysteries of Dionysus.

The *Eleusinian mysteries*, connected with the Attic city of Eleusis on the Saronic gulf, were at bottom mysteries of the reviving grain : as the grain perishes when cast into a furrow of the earth, but after dwelling a certain time under its covering, rises again, so rises again the soul of a man buried in the bosom of the earth.   This teaching found expression in a myth : Cora, the daughter of Demeter, was carried away by the ruler of the underworld ; her mother, after long and painful wanderings, discovered the place of her abode and gained thus much, that for a certain time she received back her daughter, who thereafter spent a third part of the year with her husband, and two-thirds with her mother.   She gained this by mother's love ; love and the desire for a new union with those who had departed

rather than, as is supposed, the egoism of an
individual attached to life, were in ancient
religion the source of inspiration for those who
preached the doctrine of the immortality of the
soul.   Cora, as a result of her being carried away,
learned the secrets of the underworld ; having
learned them, she revealed them to her mother.
Demeter and Cora know in what manner a man
may secure himself ' a better fate ' in the other
world ; and, since they love men, they have
consented to impart their knowledge to them
also.

With this aim they founded their mysteries
in the same city of Eleusis where for the first
time ears of grain had rustled on the fields, thanks
to an earlier act of benevolence that Demeter
had shown to humanity.   Ever since then the
initiated have met at that spot—from Eleusis,
from Attica, from all Hellas ; men and women,
rich and poor, freemen and slaves—in the
presence of the goddess all are equal.   At the
festival of the Eleusinia, originally a festival of
sowing, they gather together, worship the
goddesses with dances and songs by night on
their bright meadow by the sea, in order that
later in the temple of the mysteries (*telestērion*)
they may obtain the honour of beholding a
sacred drama, which awakens in the spectators
a certainty of the immortality of the soul and of
its ' better fate ' in the other world.   It will not
wander as a powerless and half-conscious shade

in the misty abysses of Hades—it will enter
green groves, over which cool breezes play and
on which shines the sun of our nights, it will
circle in an eternal choreia of transformed souls
and will breathe in happiness with its whole
being.

But the condition of that happiness must be
initiation : the voice of the herald summoned to
Eleusis in autumn only those who had previously been initiated into the ' lesser mysteries '
in the spring.   From this point of view one may
put the question whether the Eleusinian
mysteries had also a moral significance.   The
cynic and mocker Diogenes denied this.   ' " What
then ! " said he, " shall the condition of Pataecion,
the notorious robber, after death be better than
that of Epaminondas, merely for his being
initiated in these mysteries ? " ' (Plutarch, *How
a Young Man ought to hear Poems* : tr. Goodwin).
This is just as if some fanatic Catholic should
maintain : ' The robber Fra Diavolo, who was
christened, and who partook of communion
before his execution, will behold from the heights
of paradise how the unchristened Socrates is
tortured in the flames of Gehenna.'   One may
maintain that view as a last resort, yet St.
Augustine understood the matter otherwise.

Diogenes of Sinope had not been initiated
himself and did not know the Eleusinian teaching,
but Aristophanes of Athens knew it.   He did not
dare to make it public ; but yet he ventured,

in one of his comedies, to put into the mouths of
his chorus—a chorus of persons initiated into
the Eleusinian mysteries—the following song in
the other world :

> O happy, mystic chorus,
> The blessed sunshine o'er us
> On us alone is smiling,
>   In its soft sweet light :
> On us who strove for ever
> With holy, pure endeavour,
> Alike by friend and stranger
>   To guide our steps aright.
>
> [*Frogs*, 454-459 : tr. ROGERS.]

These words leave us no room for doubt. No,
the condition for gaining happiness in the paradise of Demeter was not single, but twofold.
Initiation was the formal religious condition, as is
baptism for a Christian. But besides this there
was a further, moral condition—a life passed in
righteousness. To those initiated at Eleusis the
Hierophant made a ' proclamation ' (*prorrhēsis*) ;
in it he excluded from the sacred choreia all those
who, though initiated, had nevertheless drawn
on themselves the wrath of the goddesses by
their sinful life—these then did not share in the
holy ceremonies ; or even if they shared in them,
they did so to their own spiritual destruction.
After death neither trial nor special punishments
were necessary ; the uninitiated throng lived
without sufferings to be sure, but lived the life of
pale phantoms in the jaws of Hades ; and only

the good, stamped with the seal of Eleusis, did the queen of the world beyond the grave take by the hand and lead into a land where began for them the Hellenic happiness—an eternal choreia on a flowery meadow, accompanied by the murmur of a gentle breeze, playing amid the rustling leaves of the poplars.

At the opening of the historic life of Greece a new cult, glaringly opposed to its constant feeling for measure and limitation, penetrated into it from the land of unruly forces and raging passions, from Thrace—the *cult of Dionysus*. In its origin it was most probably a means of influencing by magic the fertility of the earth ; and in a society marked by unbridled barbarism, sexual indulgence, as a sympathetic means, awakening the earth to fertility, was not foreign to it ; but when it passed over to the soil of orderly Hellas this element must needs fall away : there remained, as the characteristic trait of the new mysteries, *ecstasy* (*ekstasis*, literally ' a stepping out of oneself '), access to which was gained through the deafening music of tympana (that is, tambourines), cymbals, and flutes (that is, clarinets), and above all, through the bewildering ' orgiastic ' *dance*. Women were peculiarly subject to the magic of ecstasy ; hence the train of the new god was mainly composed of Bacchantes : in their ' nebrides ' (that is, fawn-skins), girt with living serpents, with thyrsi in their hands and wreaths of ivy on their loosened hair, they have remained for all time as the symbol of the beautiful savagery that sleeps in the depths of the human soul, but is beautiful only because Hellas gave beauty to it.

In the ecstasy of the dance the soul really ' stepped out ' of the bounds of the corporeal life, was transformed, learned the bliss of existence outside the body, fused with wholeness and with nature ; on the basis of his own unerring experience man became convinced of the independent existence of his soul, of the possibility for it of a life independent of the body, and therefore of its immortality : such was the eschatological meaning of the religion of Dionysus. It conquered all Greece in the eighth and seventh centuries in the whirl of an ecstatic dance.

Erwin Rohde, the best investigator of this phenomenon, convincingly compares it to the ' mania for dancing ' (*Tanzwut*) that prevailed in central Europe after the great plague of the thirteenth century. Of course the religion of Apollo, which everywhere introduced moderation, strove to do away with the excesses of the new cult : the ' orgies ' of Dionysus were confined to certain limits of time and place ; they could be held only on Parnassus and, furthermore, only once in two years (at the so-called ' trieterides '). In the rest of Greece the religion of Dionysus was modified so as to agree

with the calm forms of the public cult. The
festivals of Dionysus, as we have seen, were
brought into connection with the work of wine-
making—and traces of the ancient ecstasy were
preserved only in masquerade games, and in the
theatre of Dionysus, where it was transformed
by poetry.

This repression of the primitive religion of
Dionysus apparently occasioned a new wave of
it, which also came from Thrace, and which
was joined to the name of Orpheus, the prophet
of Dionysus. This wave also came under the
pacifying influence of the religion of Apollo :
the result of this influence was the *Orphic
mysteries*, which were composed of three parts,
cosmogonic, moral, and eschatological.

The cosmogonic part of the Orphic teaching
rested on an ancient myth that related how Zeus
conquered the Titans (compare p. 159 below)
and founded by violence the kingdom of the gods.
In order that he might transfer it from hands
defiled by violence into pure hands, Zeus made a
mother of Persephone, the queen of the depths
below the earth ; and she bore to him (the first)
Dionysus-Zagreus. The Titans enticed to themselves the little Dionysus by the temptation of a
reflection in their mirrors ; and, after enticing
him, tore him into bits and devoured him. Pallas
saved the heart and brought it to Zeus ; he,
after swallowing it, espoused Semele, the daughter of Cadmus, and she bore to him (a second)

Dionysus. And from the Titans arose the human race.

With this cosmogonic part, in which primitive Thracian savagery was so marvellously transformed by profound Greek symbolism, is joined a moral part. If we spring from the Titans, who devoured the first Dionysus, then our spiritual nature must be composed of two elements, the Titanic and the Dionysiac. The first draws us to corporality, to individuation, to all that is earthly and low; the second, on the contrary, to spirituality, to a new union in Dionysus, to all that is heavenly and lofty. Our moral duty is to suppress Titanism within us and to strive for the liberation of the spark of Dionysus that smoulders there. A means to this end was the 'Orphic life' revealed to those initiated in the Orphic mysteries. One of its duties was to refrain from animal food; this idea arose under the influence of a belief of which I shall speak in a moment.

In the nature of things, an eschatological teaching grows out of the moral teaching. The living Dionysus, the heart of Zagreus, desires a new union with all the parts of his scattered body. Therefore the aim of every man's life should be finally to set free that part of the god which lives within him, and to give it comfort in the great being of the restored Dionysus. But the road to this is very difficult. Titanism is our constant hindrance, tempting us to new

individuation and new incorporation. And so
we are born and we die, and anew we are born,
ever again and again do we enclose our soul in
' the grave of the body ' (*sōma*—*sēma*), ever
again and again do we incorporate ourselves—
among other ways even in the bodies of beasts
(this is the reason why Orpheus bids us abstain
from animal foods)—and there is no end to the
tormenting ' circle of births ' until we hear at
last the voice of Orpheus and return to the
' Orphic life '. Even then we shall not at once
be saved. Thrice must we live through a blame-
less life both here, on earth, and there, in the
kingdom of Persephone, until there shall arise
for us at last the dawn of liberation, of new
union, and of comfort.

The stay in the kingdom of Persephone before
a new incarnation is understood as a time of
purification from the sins of life ; her precincts
are for the greater part of mankind a *purgatory*.
But whoever has lived his life on earth without
sin, will enjoy happiness in that world also, in
a temporal *paradise*—until the voice of necessity
calls him back to earth for new trials. There
are, however, men who have defiled themselves
by ' incurable' crimes : for them there is no purification ; they are condemned to eternal punishment in *hell*. Therefore a *judgment beyond the
grave* awaits every soul after death : stern and
incorruptible judges must decide which of the
three realms shall be the place of its abode.

The Orphic mysteries, in distinction from those of Eleusis, were not connected with any city : everywhere in Greece, especially among the Greek colonies in the west, there arose societies of Orphics, who lived and celebrated their festivals under the guidance of their masters. It is apparent that the purity and the spiritual level of the teaching depended on the personal qualities of these last ; and even if, from this point of view, the majority of the ' Orpheotelestae ', who terrified the people by the horrors of tortures beyond the grave, occasionally aroused the mockery of enlightened men, on the other hand, earnest preachers of this doctrine found it possible to raise it to such a height that not only poets like Pindar, but even philosophers were subject to its charm. The great *Pythagoras* made Orphism the fundamental teaching of his order, a genuine masonry, which in the sixth century had its principal lodge in Croton, and from the fifth century to about the second, in Tarentum. Both through the Pythagoreans and independently of them, *Plato* also was subject to the influence of Orphism : to be sure, in the specifically dogmatic part of his teaching he makes no concessions to Orphism, but in those fantastic myths with which he has adorned his *Gorgias*, his *Phaedo*, and especially the last book of his *Republic*, he shows to a very high degree the influence of the Orphic eschatology. This influence did not end with Plato : partly by the broad river of his philosophy, but still more by underground streams, which we are partially discovering only at the present day, the Orphic eschatology penetrated even into *Christianity*. The Church sometimes strove to place in its way the dam of the Gospel, then again let it proceed unchecked, considering that certain features of it (for instance, the doctrine of purgatory) were not at variance with its own teachings, and might even be recommended by the Church. At all events Orphism to a notable degree diversified and enlivened Christian conceptions of the world beyond the grave : without Orpheus there would have been no Dante.

VII

RELIGIOUS PHILOSOPHY

A LEARNED philologist and student of Greek religion, G. F. Schömann, in his *Griechische Alterthümer* (ed. 4 : vol. ii. p. 164), after citing the introduction to the code of Zaleucus that I have quoted above (p. 122), continues as follows : ' So much the more must it amaze us that neither to Zaleucus nor to Solon nor to any other ancient lawgiver did the idea occur, nor did any one of them deem it possible to provide, that by appropriate institutions, connected with the cult, the people should be instructed truthfully and properly, and a genuine fear of God spread among them'. I give an exact translation of these words, since they show in clear-cut relief how narrow is the Christian, and in particular the Protestant, point of view, how helpless it is in the presence of so all-embracing a religion as that of Greece. I hope that to the reader who has followed attentively the course of my reasoning, these words will seem just as strange as to the author of this book. To imagine that a Greek of the epoch of Plato, who

derived an immediate revelation of the deity
from the contemplation of the Zeus of Phidias,
and from taking part in the rites of the Eleusinian festival, which had instructed him in a
spirit of true—not *fear* of God, to be sure, but
love of God—to imagine that this Greek needed
further private lessons in religion and something
in the nature of Luther's Short Catechism !

Schömann, as a Protestant, would obviously
reply that image and rite are but a parable,
while God can be truly revealed only by words.
And when, as a Protestant, he affirmed this, he
would err ; for when one speaks of God, the word
is just as much a parable as are the image and
the rite, only that it is far weaker in its effect.
The Greek was not only an intellectualist, but
the father of our intellectualism ; and yet he
understood that religion is a matter not of intellect but of feeling ; he understood something
which after the lapse of many ages his best pupil,
Goethe, was to speak forth, in the immortal
words of his Faust. Image and rite are the most
potent guides of religious feeling ; therefore I
have striven to emphasize them properly in this
treatment of Greek religion. But after giving
them sufficient space within the bounds of this
modest volume, I now pass to the third parable,
that of the word.

The need of clothing the fullness of religious
feeling in an imperfect garment of words made
its appearance early in Greece—long before

Homer. Feeling himself primarily under the rule of a religion of nature, man noticed the life of nature, full of storms, which could be understood either as a struggle or as a development. Light struggles with darkness, warmth struggles with cold—yes, but to an equal degree the day emerges from the night, the summer emerges from the winter. These two conceptions offered man the two fundamental parables of his later mythology: the parable of struggle, and hence of discord; and the parable of birth, and hence of the union of the sexes. Uranus (Heaven), by fructifying Earth, begets the Titans and the Titanids, the representatives of the unbridled forces of nature. Earth, bending beneath the weight of her own fruits, implores the aid of Cronus, the youngest of the Titans; and at her request he deprives his father of generative power. Later, uniting with the Titanid Rhea (a second hypostasis of that same Earth), Cronus himself begets a powerful generation of gods; foreseeing that this generation will be his destruction, he swallows his own children; but Rhea saves one of them, Zeus. Zeus in the struggles of the worlds conquers Cronus and the Titans, and, casting them down into Tartarus, founds his own kingdom, in which we are living. To be sure, retribution awaits him also, and a son will be born to him who will be more powerful than he; Zeus himself is fated to meet defeat in a struggle with the regenerated forces of Earth, the Giants. We have already seen (p. 152) how the cosmogony of Orphism rests on this cosmogony. The religion of Apollo took a different attitude with regard to it, proclaiming the reconciliation of Earth to Zeus and the eternity of the kingdom of Zeus, and doing away with the nightmare of the ' gigantomachia '—yet not completely : the ancient dread slumbered on in the impression-able souls of the people—and even in the first century after Christ, when the cloud that overwhelmed Pompeii arose from Vesuvius, the Greeks of the Neapolitan land clearly distin-guished in its fantastic outlines the monstrous forms of the Titans, who were returning from Tartarus through the jaws of the fiery mountain, in order to devour the kingdom of gods and men.

This ' theogony ', the strange product of dim antiquity, was preserved to historic times in the poem of Hesiod. What was to be done with it ? Long before that time men had become con-vinced of the revelation of God in goodness, and there was precious little goodness in this mythology of struggles between son and father and sexual unions of brother and sister. . . . What was to be done ? The same thing that was done with the ancient statues made by Daedalus, when the Zeus of Phidias was already in exis-tence : while revering the imperfect revelations of a dusky past, to nourish one's soul on the more perfect revelations of more recent times.—Yes, but they were injurious : Aristophanes in his *Clouds* has shown clearly how the Sophists took advantage of them in order to overthrow the very idea of justice :

> *Wrong Logic.*   If Justice be there,
> How comes it that Zeus could his father reduce,
> Yet live with their godships unpunished and loose?

But was there anything of which the Sophists did not take advantage ! And in Aristophanes the opponent of the speaker makes the only proper reply to him, pointing out the nauseating character of his reasoning :

> *Right Logic.* Ugh ! Ugh ! These evils come thick,
>   I feel awfully sick :
> A basin, quick, quick !
>   [*Clouds*, 904-907 : tr. ROGERS.]

Yet the point is that neither the *Theogony* of Hesiod nor any other ancient book was canonical. We possess religious feeling : what it does not hesitate to accept is true, the rest is non-existent for us.

To be sure, even in the epoch of Socrates, there were men who interpreted in their own fashion the ancient myths of the conflicts among the gods and were of the opinion that in this interpretation they might be accepted. Plato introduces us to such a theologian in the person of Euthyphro, a very peculiar man and in his own way a deep thinker. To him Socrates replies : ' May not this be the reason, Euthyphro, why

I am charged with impiety—that I cannot away with these stories [of discord and violence] about the gods?' (*Euthyphro*, 6 A: tr. Jowett.)

This reply was made under the impression of the accusation which caused the death of the Athenian sage, and therefore it breathes forth a bitterness which Athens did not deserve; in the most anxious times of the Peloponnesian War Euripides had expressed with impunity the same thought through the lips of his Heracles :

> I deem not that the gods for spousals crave
> Unhallowed : tales of gods' hands manacled
> Ever I scorned, nor ever will believe,
> Nor that one god is born another's lord.
> For god hath need, if god indeed he be,
> Of naught : these be the minstrels' sorry tales.
>
> [*Heracles*, 1341-46 : tr. WAY.]

But let us leave the Daedali of the revelation in the word and come to its masters, men of the same rank as Phidias and Praxiteles. By concentrating our attention on the Athens of the fourth and third centuries, we may free ourselves from the necessity of following the *history* of Greek religious philosophy through the doctrines of the Ionians, the Eleatics, Empedocles, and the Sophists : they survived at that period only in so far as they were regenerated in Plato and others. If we have made an exception for the oldest theogony, it is only because that maintained itself on the surface, living in the poems of Homer and, above all, in those of Hesiod.

In accordance with what has been said above, we shall have to deal with the *parable* of Plato, Aristotle, the Stoa, and Epicurus, with the symbolic utterance of the unutterable. All these sages work with the chisel of their logos, striving for such perfection as is possible for them; they are all justified by the honesty of their intellectual toil. In this honesty one element is their consciousness of the limits of their own logos, a consciousness of the fundamental unprovability of what they say, and their consequent *tolerance*. And this tolerance doubly justifies them.

One thing more I must point out at the outset. Our own religious scholasticism long ago established, and termed fundamental, a division of religions into monotheistic religions and polytheistic religions, and applied the adjective *imperfect* to the latter, in comparison with the former: this in turn has given it the right to place even the religion of Islam in a higher position than that of Pericles, Sophocles, and their fellow Athenians—that is, to reach an absurd conclusion. A reader who has become imbued with this notion is usually much surprised when he sees that the Greek writers whom I have mentioned above do not once put the question of monotheism and polytheism. That question had long ago been crossed off the slate by Greek religion. How many Muses are there: one or many? How many Graces (Charites)?

How many Erinyes ? Better yet : at Olympia a system of twelve deities was recognized ; one altar was consecrated to Zeus and Posidon, one to Hera and Athena, and so on—and finally, one to Dionysus and the Charites. ' Therefore,' Schömann informs us (vol. ii. p. 142), ' since there were several of these last, the number twelve was in point of fact exceeded '. This actually amounts to saying that the Greeks did not know how to count.

In reality, however, they felt to perfection that in the domain of divinity unity is fused with plurality, and this feeling makes their religious consciousness not lower but higher than our scholasticism. In the domain of discursive reasoning the school of the Eleatics worked out the problem : it came to the conclusion that unity exists, but as something ineffable, something bereft of all active energy ; it becomes active only after passing through the prism of plurality. For a thinking man, therefore, the question whether the Greek religion was monotheistic or polytheistic ceases to exist.

That religion was both monotheistic and polytheistic also in the philosophy of *Plato*, who bound together god or the gods with humanity in so firm a union on the basis of his lofty doctrine of the ' ideas '. To be sure, he did not at once reach those summits of metaphysics. He is very sensitive to the beauty of the visible world, to the immortality of the species living in it ; his Eros is a divine force, uniting in ecstasy individuals of different sexes for the purpose of the continuance of the species : ' Love is the desire for birth in beauty in order to gain immortality ' (*Symposium*, 206 E). Thus does he understand the prophetess Diotima's deep doctrine of love. Yet he has a feeling for a beauty higher than the beauty of the visible world, he soars above that world on the wings of Orphism—and here the body seems to him as but the prison of the soul, and death as its liberation.   The true habitation of the soul is the domain of Hades ; here it will gain a fullness of the forces that are weakened by the lusts of the body, a swiftness of sight that is dimmed by corporality. . . .

No, not the domain of Hades, but the expanse above the heavens.   Here in radiant immobility abide the perfect models of that which only seemed to us perfect on earth ; here abide the eternal ' ideas,' the contemplation of which is the true food of immortality both for the gods and for the soul.   The gods, thanks to the perfection of their nature, enjoy it without hindrance, and so they are immortal by nature.   But our souls are chariots, each of which is harnessed to two steeds, the steed of the strong will and the steed of sensual lust, and is guided by the charioteer of reason.   And when, accompanying the journey of the gods through the realm of the ideas, above the heavens, souls strive to devote themselves to their contemplation, in order that they too may enjoy the food of immortality, the steed of sensual lust obstinately draws them downward into the domain of the mist beneath the heavens, and for many souls it becomes the cause of downfall.

So they abide upon earth, locked in the prison of their bodies : yet they have brought with them a remembrance of what they beheld in the realm of the ideas above the heavens— except for those unhappy and ruined souls which, owing to the uncontrolled violence with which the steeds of sensuality drew them to earth, could observe nothing. They are fettered by longing for the paradise that they have seen and lost. This longing is peculiarly strong when on earth they encounter the reflection of a heavenly idea ; but, swaddled with the wrappings of the body, it is only through the senses that they can recognize those earthly reflections. And since of all the senses the sense of sight acts most effectively on us, therefore we are filled with the greatest ardour by the *visual* reflection of the idea, or beauty, earthly beauty. This is why the soul of man in the presence of beauty feels the strongest long- ing, an uncontrollable longing ; we term that feeling love, and it seems to us that love strives for the possession of a beloved being : but that is not true. It strives for that idea above the heavens, the reflection of which the soul sees in the beloved being ; and under its influence the soul takes on holiness, its lost wings grow anew, the soul regains the capacity for a return, after throwing off the fetters of the body, to its habitation above the heavens.

This is obviously only a parable—also only a reflection of a divine idea hovering before the eyes of the prophet's soul.   But this parable of Platonic love has always possessed and still possesses in the highest degree that capacity which the prophet himself ascribed to the most perfect reflections in the visible world of the beauty above the heavens—the capacity of giving wings to our soul and of directing its flight, above the mists of visibility, to its tabernacle above the heavens.

And the gods ?
A reader of Plato notes, not without amazement, that they play a rather secondary part in this duality of worlds.   Eternal are the ideas that abide above the heavens, eternal and inviolable is the law of their reflection in material beneath the heavens, eternal also is the very material that receives the stamp of the ideas.   God is not its creator : he is only the master that shapes it, an artisan—a ' demiourgos '.

Plato's teaching here depends on two fundamental doctrines of the ' Daedalian ' philosophy of religion ; we have not yet had an opportunity to speak of them and must now atone for the omission.

The first is the *idea of fate* and of the depen-

dence of the gods on it. It appears most forcibly
in the oldest parts of Homer, which do not admit
divine omnipotence : Zeus weighs on the scales
of Moira the destiny of men and cannot give aid
to a man condemned by Moira. Later follows
a strengthening of the conception of divine
omnipotence, the crown of which is the words
in the *Odyssey* (x. 306) : ' The gods can do all '.
Henceforward Moira is nothing else than the
will of the gods and of Zeus ; the gods and Zeus
assign her to men : the primeval spinner as of
old spins the thread of man's life, but the god
guides her toil. This conception wins its utmost
power in the religion of Apollo :

To men I will make known the unerring will of Zeus—
[*Homeric Hymn to Apollo*, 132]

the first-born son of the ruler of Olympus proclaims at his birth.

. . . But what is Moira ? In my opinion, the
knowledge and the prophetic power of Earth,
or of nature : the Russian critic Pisarev was very
near the truth when he saw in her a personification of the law of causality. The authority of
Moira over Zeus is the natural correspondent
of the idea of the supremacy of primeval Earth
over Zeus, who was born in time and who
trembles at the thought of his own destruction
at the hands of the Giants. So this authority
vanished when Apollo proclaimed that Zeus
also was eternal both in the past and in the
future.

It vanished, but not entirely : the older parts
of the *Iliad* were still a part of the popular consciousness—no canon had proclaimed them
heretical ; and while Greek religion lives, the
idea of divine omnipotence is in constant rivalry
with the idea of the authority of Moira over the
gods. If a Christian thinks that his religion has
overcome this rivalry, let him try to answer the
childish question whether God can bring it to
pass that two and two make something else
than four.

Religious thought in the sixth and fifth centuries made profit of this rivalry in its own way.
The gods rule over men, but over the gods rules
law (nomos). For this very reason the thought
of that time was reconciled to polytheism even
on the basis of popular conceptions. The
' irresistible ' argument of Mohammed, that polytheism would lead to anarchy, it would have
recognized as fully worthy of his barbaric intellect, which had never known a law-abiding city-
state *(polis).* Yet if even man, the more perfect
he becomes, the more willingly subordinates
himself to civic law, what shall we think of the
most perfect of the perfect, the gods ?

Next—*matter* with its primeval existence :
here too we recognize that same Earth, only
expanded and logically—not actually—deified.
The fact must be emphasized that the Greek in
the most illustrious epochs of his history never
even for a moment supposed that god could

create the earth, that is, matter, out of nothing.
To be sure, the *Theogony* of Hesiod seems to
imply that before Earth (and Uranus, the
heavens) there was chaos ; but that is only a
figure of speech, nothing more.   Chaos in Hesiod
means ' a yawning mouth '.   The Greek carried
out consistently a conception which in some
modern languages is expressed in a comparison
of the heavens to the palate : thus Polish *niebo*,
heavens ; and *podniebienie,* palate.   The world
is as it were a mouth.   The palate corresponds
to the heavens (in Greek *ouranos* has both
meanings) ; the earth is the tongue, a flat disk
in space ; the lower jaw, if you wish, is Tartarus.
Let us imagine that there is neither earth,
nor heavens (nor Tartarus)—what will remain ?
Chaos : that is, a mouth, a yawning void,
nothingness.   That is what Hesiod means.   But
never did it occur to his thoughts that any
being by his magisterial word created the heavens
and the earth out of nothing, out of a void.

Later speculation again took advantage in its
own way of Hesiod's concepts of ' chaos ' and
' Earth '.   It understood literally, and not figura-
tively, their sequence in time : consequently to
the word ' chaos ' a new meaning must be given,
the same one to which we are accustomed.
' Chaos ' is disorderly matter ; its opposite is
' cosmos ', matter in a state of order.   So there
was an act that brought about order in matter ;
the author of that act is god.

Such is the view of Plato ; here we will not enter into details.

As the creator of the order of the world, however, god has to deal with passive matter, resistant in its passivity. He himself, as the being who has introduced system, is the source of good and only of good, as the sun is the source only of light and of warmth. . We call dark and cold those parts of matter which have not yet received a sufficient portion of the sun's light and warmth ; in exactly the same way an insufficient penetration of that same spiritualized matter by the force of good, we call *evil*.

The gods are mediators between the ideas and men. All the ideas are subject to one, the idea of good ; the good gods foster good among men, never evil. And you, poets, as teachers of the people, should enlighten it in precisely that spirit. If you wish to represent in your works that the gods also send down evil to men, you may do so, but you must needs indicate that this apparent evil, sufferings and the like, has good as its highest aim. In the good lies the justification of all that proceeds from the gods.

The gods, moreover, when they communicate with men, themselves employ mediators to that end ; these mediators are the *daemons*. In the religious philosophy of Plato this concept, the meaning of which is uncertain in the popular faith, receives a definite sense of lower, media-tive forces. Every man has his daemon, his guardian spirit, whom he received at birth, or even before his birth ; there exist also daemons in general, the messengers of the gods. These bear to the gods the prayers of men and to men the sentences of the gods ; all the region beneath the heavens is full of daemons.

As a daemon also we must regard that being at whose mysterious touch a man who has beheld earthly beauty, strives towards that beauty which he once beheld in his habitation above the heavens, in consequence of which his soul receives wings and gains the capacity to return whence it came. Love is the first and the last word of Plato's philosophy.

Penetrated through and through with the murmur of poetry, all trembling from the joyous emotion of an ardent soul, the philosophy of Plato by the potent force of its charm called together men of kindred temperament beneath the rustling plane trees of Academus, until, after many generations, it produced a temporary reaction in the shape of the sharp scepticism of Arcesilaüs and the school of the ' Middle Academy ' ; of this, as sterile in matters of religion, we shall say nothing. All may be included in two words : ancient Voltairianism.

But before this time, in the grove of the Lycean Apollo, there blazed forth another torch of religious thought, which was lighted by a pupil of Plato, faithful and loving, but not an

enthusiast, only a sober and judicious man,
Aristotle. ' Of two friends, Plato and the truth,
one must prefer the truth.' (Compare *Ethics*,
i. 4.)   The truth, *his* truth, was as follows :

Life is motion : all that lives moves : the
source of motion we call deity.   Deity is moved
by no one, for if it were moved, it would have a
source of motion outside itself and of itself
would not be motion ; but, not being moved, it
nevertheless moves, for it lives.   It is moved by
itself and it moves itself ; in it and only in it
the active and the passive capacity for motion
form a unit.   But the world is moved by the
deity, which therefore must be in touch with it.
(' Gravitation ' Aristotle would not have understood ; and, to speak perfectly frankly, neither
do we understand it.)   The deity is in touch with
the world, abiding in the expanse above the
heavens, immediately beyond the ' firmament ',
or first and most perfectly moved sphere of the
cosmos.   There are many of these spheres and
there are many gods who set them in motion,
and who derive their strength to move them
from the supreme deity ; therein lies the truth
of the popular parable of polytheism.

But what externally appears as motion,
internally is *thought* ; the supreme deity, the
source of motion, is also the source of thought,
is the supreme *reason*.   Here too the active
and the passive capacity form a unit : deity
thinks itself and is thought by itself.   And in

consequence of its supreme perfection, thought
and will, which are divided in man, also form a
unit in it. In man will is directed towards
what seems to him beauty—but to the deity
nothing can seem : the object of his thought
and will is true beauty. This beauty the deity
realizes through thought and will—realizes it
in the cosmos, which it moves.

Herein lies the supreme *happiness* of the deity ;
again the popular parable speaks the truth, when
it recognizes the gods not only as immortal,
but as happy. Man, however, cannot conceive
of this happiness. Only at times, excessively
rarely, do we succeed, by the exertion of all our
powers of thought, in burying ourselves within
ourselves, so that we begin to live by reason—
and for us those are moments of incomparable
happiness ; but the deity experiences this happiness always and eternally.

It thinks itself, its perfect beauty ; and thinking it, it strives towards it by will ; and striving
towards it by will, it realizes it in the cosmos
which it moves, in accord with the aim of the
universe, which it thinks. This realization
depends on the interpenetration of *matter* by
deity. Deity and matter—again that same
primordial dualism, the Zeus and the Earth of
the popular parable. Just as deity is primeval,
so is matter—the idea of the creation of the world
from nothing is foreign to Aristotle, as it is
equally foreign, and organically so, to the healthy

Greek reason in general.   Neither the deity nor matter had a beginning, and hence their motion also had no beginning.   Deity is the cause, but not the beginning of motion.

Here something is involved which is unintelligible for us, and organically so.   The philosophy of Aristotle leads to evolutionism, but evolutionism not in time, but merely in causality. Let us humble ourselves and be reconciled to this.

Matter (*hylē*), which of itself is bereft of qualities and forms, possesses an unlimited capacity for acquiring them ; it is then unlimited *possibility* (*dynamis, potentia*).   In it therefore are *potentially* (dynamically) included all qualities and all forms ; the gradual realization of these qualities and forms, the transfer of them from potentiality to actuality or *energy*, transfers matter itself from a state bereft of qualities and forms to a state possessing qualities and forms of *being* (*ousia, substantia*).

Gradual realization—but, I repeat, gradual not in time.   The first stage is the four elements, two extreme (earth with its striving downward and fire with its striving upward) and two intermediate.   The second stage is inorganic nature.   In the next stage appears the soul, in which and through which the further gradation is developed.   The *vegetative* soul is capable of growth and reproduction.   The *animal* soul is capable of sensual perception.   And finally—

always omitting transitional forms—the *human* soul is capable of thought, possesses *reason*.

Reason is then the kernel of the human soul in its vegetative-animal nature; in that soul it acts in more or less the same way that the divine reason acts in matter. Reason itself also, as reason, is of divine origin, is a spark of that supreme fire above the heavens. So it is not subject to dissolution and death. Though the deductions of Aristotle as to the fate of the soul after the death of the body are distinguished by extreme caution and moderation—Luther even concluded from them that Aristotle denied the immortality of the soul, and cursed him for it— yet it is evident that he limits mortality to the vegetative-animal nature of the human soul. Set free from its fetters, the divine reason returns to its source and unites anew with it in harmonious, mighty being; in this manner Aristotle incorporated in his philosophy the profound parable of the Orphic religion.

But even during life, thanks to the presence in the soul of a spark of reason, man is a creature akin to the deity. Reason makes him capable of the highest sort of virtue, of *dianoetic* virtue, distinct from *ethical* virtue, which rests on native qualities and unconscious habit; reason also at times permits him to tear himself free from the gravitation of his vegetative-animal soul, to bury himself within himself and through *internal* contemplation (*theōria*) to have an early taste of the final happiness, when, united anew with his source above the heavens, he shall share in its thought of the eternal, indestructible beauty.

A house and garden by the Dipylon Gate in Athens at the beginning of the third century ; a modest house and a modest garden. From that house faithful friends carry forth on warm days a man incurably ill, that the gentle air and the gentle sun may soothe his sufferings. Then the sick man expounds to them the philosophy of his sickness.

It is *Epicurus*.

All depends on the body ; there is naught in the world except the body and bodies. The body is formed by the gathering and cohesion of atoms of various forms. The smoothest of them compose what we call the soul ; entering our body, thanks to their smoothness, they support its cohesion and are themselves supported by it in cohesion—for a certain time. Death, the severance of soul and body, brings with it the dissolution of both : the slow dissolution of the body and the immediate dissolution of the soul. The immortality of the soul is an empty dream.

The world likewise is a body, a collection of the bodies of which it is composed ; it arose in the course of time through the gathering and cohesion of those same atoms, and in the course of time will similarly dissolve and perish. And not it alone, but all worlds, however many there may be.

And the gods ?   Obviously they exist, seeing
that everybody recognizes their existence—
here the discursive reasoning of Epicurus the
individual bows before a universal intuition.
They are just such beings as all men recognize
them to be : in the first place, immortal ; in
the second, happy. Obviously they are also
corporeal and consequently are composed of
atoms, yet they possess the capacity of doing
eternally what we men can do only temporally ;
that is, of renewing their being by separating
certain atoms from themselves and acquiring
others.   The worlds do not possess that capacity,
and so they are not the dwelling of the gods.
The gods dwell in the *spaces between the worlds*—
as it were in quiet oases between the storms of
the worlds.   And seeing that they are happy, it
follows—and here the gaze of the sick man rested
with love and sorrow on his friends, who, full
of anxiety, observed the symptoms of the return
of his sufferings—it follows that they are free
from cares for the human race and for the world
in general.   Therefore the world and the human
race are abandoned entirely to the mechanical
action of their atoms, entirely governed by two
blind forces, necessity and chance.

Not entirely. The world is, to be sure ; but
besides this, man possesses free will, or, to speak
more exactly, the power of choice (*prohairesis*),
which makes it possible for him to gain what is
best from situations created for him by necessity

and chance. This did not follow logically from the mechanistic premises of the sage, but it followed as an obvious inference from the manliness with which he surmounted his illness, from the gentle and kindly smile with which he endured its torturing attacks.

At all events man is left to himself ; the gods, taking no part in the founding of the universe, do not trouble themselves about it. *There is no divine providence.* This results inevitably from the fundamental premise of the happiness of the gods, and just as inevitably from our experience of life. Would the prosperity of the evil be possible, or—here again the sight of the sufferings of the master excluded the possibility of an objection—the misery of the good, if the gods really troubled themselves about our lot ?

For the time being let us also refrain from objections, and think through to the end the thought of Epicurus. Is this a religion or the negation of religion ? Epicurus recognizes the existence of the gods : they are immortal, happy, even anthropomorphic, since ' seeing that the human form is the most perfect of all, it is impossible to suppose that the gods have preferred to it any other '. Yet at the same time Epicurus deprives them of all share in the government of the world and of the fate of man ; he removes them to the solitary islands of the spaces between the worlds. What cult is possible under such conditions ? Why offer prayers that will not be heard ? Why make sacrifices and observe festivals that give no joy to those whose worship they serve ? And what is a religion without a cult ?

Here a contemptuous smile flitted over the lips of the sage. ' Yes, men, that is like you : you wish to derive profit from your divine service. But for us it is needless. We worship the gods as models of perfection, as higher beings, untouched by the impermanence and transitoriness of the world. We share in your prayers, sacrifices, and festivals ; but, in distinction from you, we do it disinterestedly.'

As the reader sees, the kernel of the religious philosophy of Epicurus is the idea of *divine providence*—or, to speak more exactly, its negation. Neither Plato nor Aristotle would agree with him. In Plato god, the source of all good for men, distinctly gives them a helping hand, acting through his servants the daemons ; in Aristotle he does this mediately, realizing in the universe his premeditated aim of beauty and goodness. Least of all would they agree with the arguments brought forward by Epicurus. There are two of them : the argument from above and the argument from below. From above : the happiness of the gods, which it is alleged cannot be reconciled with care. Verily this is a philosophy of illness ! Happiness for a healthy man is inherent in strength and its employment, in activity and energy, in the realization of a great aim. Even the strong man has his weakness :

he needs some one who needs him.   But without this weakness there would be no strength, and likewise there would be no happiness.

The argument from below : the prosperity of the evil and the misery of the good.   The objections of Plato and of Aristotle I shall consider below ; at present I shall indicate the basis which only could lend support alike to those objections and to the argument itself.   The reader has not forgotten that complete, happy consciousness which in the epoch of the greatest power of the Greek spirit anticipated even the very possibility of the argument of Epicurus—he has not forgotten *phylonomism*.   So now I must add that at the end of the fifth century, the time of Euripides, phylonomism begins to decline.   It still maintains itself among average men, finding support in state institutions to which in former times it had given occasion ; but it was counteracted by all the doctrines that proclaimed the worth of the individual soul, not excepting those of the Academy and the Lyceum.   The sickness of Epicurus did not permit him to found a family ; this branch condemned to wither aimlessly had no feeling of solidarity with young shoots such as it was not fated to produce.   Improperly generalizing his philosophy of illness, Epicurus counselled other men also not to found a family, that source of continual cares—and cares were what his sick soul most feared.   It is clear that he stood firmly and entirely on the basis of ontonomism.

. . . The strength of the philosophy of Epicurus is not in its religious aspect ; it is in his physics, in an atomism, unoriginal to be sure, but independently comprehended and developed, which after many metamorphoses still lives to-day, as the fundamental theory of physics and chemistry. But for the development of religious thought Epicureanism, very influential in the course of the last centuries of Greece, had only a negative importance. Its aesthetic supplement, the recognition that the gods existed and should be worshipped, was not immediately occasioned by the atomistic theory as such ; it had no great weight with the masters of Epicureanism and was completely ignored by their pupils and by common men. It was hard to conceive of the gods without divine providence ; for the most part the Epicureans after all were atheists, and by their atheism attracted some men and repelled others.

In the very centre of Athens, on the market-place, rose a building which the city of Pallas might rightly regard as a monument of its heroism ; it was a hall with a colonnade, called the Painted Stoa (Porch). Built in the fifth century by a hero of the Persian Wars, Cimon, the son of Miltiades, it was adorned at his recommendation with frescoes representing the heroic combats of the Athenians in times both mythical and historical. In our epoch, when in the hospital atmosphere of the garden by the Dipylon Gate there bloomed the feeble flower of the religious philosophy of Epicurus, the heroic Stoa on the market-place at last received a soul in the form of a philosophy of heroism—the philosophy of the Stoa, as it was usually called, or *Stoicism*.

To be sure, in its doctrine of the deity the Stoa is little different from the Lyceum ; each sect may with equal propriety be called both monotheistic and polytheistic—something which is quite natural for consistent religious thought, unfettered by the chains of worship of words. The deity in its essence is one, but its manifestations are many. More strongly than Aristotle the Stoa emphasizes the materiality of this one deity ; but of course its matter is of the most subtle sort, *fire*, and moreover not elemental but ethereal fire, which is both the principle of motion and reason. In the form of fire it interpenetrates the whole universe, vivifying it and spiritualizing it ; the Stoic religion is a *pantheism*. And, moreover, it is an *evolutionary* pantheism : interpenetrating the matter of the universe, fire conducts it to ever higher forms. Here we have no need to humble ourselves ; in agreement with our own mode of thought, the Stoa recognizes evolution in time, and not merely in causality.

Fire, the soul of the universe—why not call it Zeus ?—forms, first of all, the four elements, which are likewise living and divine : earth—Demeter, water—Posidon, air—Hera, and (elemental) fire—Hephaestus. Within the elements

there exist other divine forms, and above all
the heavenly bodies : the sun—Apollo, and the
moon—Artemis. As the reader sees, the Greek
religion profited by the fact that it was in its
foundations a religion of nature : thanks to this
primary quality it entered entirely into the Stoic
system, was entirely justified by it. But not
only as a religion of nature : Zeus is likewise
the supreme reason and the entire fullness of the
divine being in beauty, goodness, and truth ; and
the individual gods, as his reflections in matter,
share in these qualities of his. Thus in the *fire*
of the Stoic system the Greek popular religion
attained its summit in the realm of thought,
just as in its ritual it attained its summit in the
realm of feeling.

A spark of the divine reason is the *rational
soul*, which is incorporated in man, to be sure,
not at the moment of conception and not at the
moment of birth : an infant is irrational, the
counterpart of a beast ; its soul is only *psychē*
and not *pneuma*. Man breathes in his rational soul
only gradually, from the atmosphere, in which it
is spread abroad ; but, breathing it in, he indi-
vidualizes it in accordance with his own inclina-
tions, impressing on it his own stamp, owing to
which it cannot after death dissolve in the essence
of the divine reason, but preserves its being, as
an individual. As may be seen from this, the
Stoa has an attitude towards individuation
fundamentally different from that of the trans-

formed Orphism of Aristotle's teaching : individuation is not an evil, but a good, and a man should prize his traits as an individual, if they are good. Stoicism is the most individualistic of the philosophic doctrines of antiquity.

Therefore it is fundamentally ontonomic. Consequently the problem of Job rises before it in all its might. The evil man fares well and the good man ill, and for this there is neither justification in the life of past generations nor recompense in the life of those to come ; each man answers for himself, each life forms a whole with its own beginning and end.   Where then is the justice of divine providence ?

Perchance in the *life beyond the grave* ?

Perchance. Stoicism recognizes that life, and moreover, in the spirit of popular religion, for each soul separately. The soul is individually immortal ; a judgment awaits it after it has abandoned the earthly realm, and after the judgment both reward and punishment. The famous ' Dream of Scipio ', which forms the conclusion of Cicero's *Republic*, gives us a decidedly majestic picture of the Stoic paradise, a picture which enraptured many men even in Christian times. However—whoever wishes, let him believe ; whoever does not wish, let him not believe. Stoicism, being also in this regard akin to the religion of Apollo, recognizes a world beyond the grave, but does not insist on details.

How shall we answer the question why the

evil man fares well and the good man ill ?   By
a denial of the question itself.   This is the very
subject on which, following indications given by
Plato, the Stoa develops its lofty ethics.   It is
not true that the evil man fares well and the good
man ill.   ' Well ' means ' in possession of good ',
' ill ' means ' in deprivation of good '.   And there
is but one good—' virtue ' ; the good man possesses it always, the evil man—never.   *Virtue
itself by itself suffices for a happy life.*

This is the philosophy of heroism.

Stoicism and Epicureanism rule men's minds
in the course of the four centuries preceding and
following the birth of Christ, and in that epoch
not Greece but Rome was the arena of human
culture.   Here then we may survey the fruits
that the two doctrines produced, and by this test
verify their worth : I think that this is a decisive
test.   Epicureanism produced at its best mild
aesthetes such as Atticus and Maecenas ; and at
its worst, selfish squanderers of the chance gift
of a life bereft of deity.   But Stoicism produced
Cato, Brutus, Thrasea, Seneca, Marcus Aurelius
—all those famous men who by their life and by
their death bore witness to the virtue dwelling
in their souls.   Stoicism verily found its justification : not only in the cold shadow of the
Painted Porch, but in the scorching arena of
life it was the philosophy of heroism.

VIII

THE REVELATION OF GOD IN TRUTH

LIKE the other two supreme revelations of God, his revelation in truth is a derivatory phenomenon in the development of the religious thought of humanity. Homer is still far enough away from it. God in Homer, in the first place, does not even always possess the truth : his knowledge is at first just as limited as his power ; and only in the *Odyssey* does Homer proclaim the principle, ' The gods know all ', along with the principle, ' The gods can do all '. Still less does god feel the necessity for announcing nothing but the truth. Zeus sends down to Agamemnon a deceitful dream ; Pallas in mortal form tempts Pandarus with a fancied prospect of success to break the truce by a treacherous shot ; and this same Pallas, appearing in mortal form to her favourite Odysseus, listens with a tender smile to his fictitious narrative of his own adventures, and later makes herself known to him and in kindly fashion forgives him his deceit, confessing that even she herself is fond of trickery.

But as the sun disperses the mist, so the

beams of Apollo in the eighth, seventh, and sixth
centuries destroy in human consciousness all
thought of the possibility of connecting the two
concepts *deity* and *lying*. 'A lie thou mayst
not touch,' says Pindar (*Pyth*. ix. 75), the prophet of Apollo, concerning his god, and moreover he understands by a 'lie' not only sub-
jective but even objective departure from truth.
Truth and *light* are, as it were, mutually correspondent concepts; Apollo rules over both of
them, and after him the rest of the gods as well.
In this field of religion, as well as in others, the
Pythagorean school, the enlightener of Hellas
in the sixth century, did fruitful work. To the
master himself is ascribed the remarkable answer
to the question, ' When is man most like god ? '
—' When he speaks the truth.'

But since the poems of Homer after all
remained current, and through them wanton
fancies as to the frivolous attitude of the gods
towards the truth might filter into the popular
consciousness, therefore Plato in his *Republic*
states energetically that they must not be tolerated. No, where god is, there is no place for
lying. God cannot err, for he knows all ; he
cannot clothe his words in the garment of lying
or his form in the garment of deceit, for in his
whole being he is truth and nothing but truth.
And if we conceive of Pan in a double form, this
has a symbolic sense—Pan is the word (*logos*).
And the word has a double form, being both

truthful and lying, abiding by its true essence on the heights in communion with the gods, and by its lying essence in a lower sphere, which alone corresponds to its ' goatish ' nature. . . . In the original we have a play on words : ' goatish ' is in Greek *tragikos*, ' tragic ' ; by the choice of this term Plato alludes to mythology, which has warped men's conception of the gods.

Yes, god is truth, possesses truth and proclaims the truth.   In god is truth and in truth is god.

We must thoroughly assimilate this conviction, which is obviously in complete accord with the teaching of every religion of a higher type.   We must join with it still another conviction, also perfectly natural for us as Christians, that god *loves* the human race and cares for it.   Then we shall perhaps understand—not the origin, but the obstinate persistence, even in the minds of the most cultivated men, of that beautiful but sterile flower of Greek religion which is called *mantic* or divination.

Not the origin, I repeat.   In fact mantic, as such, is older than either of the convictions which later became its basis.   In its primitive forms it has small connection with religion. Let us recall our own system of various and sundry *omens* : a vein twitches on my right temple—' What does that signify ? '—I stub my foot on the threshold as I leave the house—a

snake crosses my path—somebody sneezes—and
so on. Here, on the one hand, we have a naïve
empiricism, the observed repetition of certain
events after certain signs; on the other, a
seeming analogy with something which is important for our life in nature, and which we call
prognostication : the swallows are flying high—
that forebodes fair weather. The imperfection
of science does not yet enable man to distinguish
phenomena the connection of which is only
enigmatic from other phenomena the connection
of which is totally impossible ; all alike merge
in a general mist of fragments of nature and of
life that have a mysterious influence upon one
another.

In our own epoch cultivated men have recognized that the mantic of omens belongs to the
domain of superstition ; Theophrastus, in his
Character of the ' superstitious ' man (*deisidai-
mon*), regards it in the proper light. Quite
another thing is *religious* mantic. It would
obviously be possible to include even the mantic
of omens under this rubric: for who knows
what means the god who loves us may employ
to caution us against a fatal decision ? Evidently the boundary line is very indistinct ;
and if any man should wish to violate common
sense and heed all the countless omens that he
encounters, and thereby to change his life into
a hell—nobody forbids him. But a rational
man is saved by his mere common sense.

Leaving aside both the mantic of omens and another mantic, different from it but equally low, the mantic of charms of all sorts—by means of a sieve, of meal, of the pecking of grain by a hen, and so on—let us turn to that which had an evident and universally recognized connection with religion.   It had two branches, ' atechnic ' mantic or *prophesying*, and ' entechnic ' mantic or *augury*.   In the first case the god addresses man immediately, in the second he sends him signs that require interpretation by an experienced augur.   Of course, there could be no exact boundary between them ; the mantic most widely known in antiquity—and in our own times also—that of *prophetic dreams*, occupied an intermediate position, since dreams were frequently symbolic and required a soothsayer to interpret them.

Let us begin with dreams.   If we have dreamed of a dead man, it is plain that his own soul has visited us : having learned the secrets of the underworld, it has become prophetic, and if it is kindly disposed towards us we may rely on its words.   If we dream of a living man, this may be interpreted by the supposition that the god has created his phantom and has sent him to us as the god's own messenger ; and in such a case his words are equally credible. But it is also possible that an actual Dream has assumed his form, and then the matter becomes complicated.   For Dreams dwell in the same

abode as the souls, in the underworld : by day,
like bats, they slumber in a grotto ; by night they
fly forth, whether at the suggestion of one of the
souls who are their neighbours, or of their own
free will, and appear to men in their sleep.
Such is the famous Morpheus, so called because
he likes to assume the ' forms ' of men. At all
events one cannot entirely depend on such
dreams ; evidently, like the daemons, the
Dreams can proclaim the truth—but the problem is whether they will choose to do so. It
all depends on the question through which ' gate '
the Dreams have flown forth : unfortunately
there are two such gates—and if I add, ' one of
horn and the other of ivory ', my reader must
translate these terms into the Greek language
in order to understand why the Dreams are
credible when they fly through the first, and not
so when they fly through the second. But
since they do not inform us through which gate
they have flown to us, then—   Therefore
Euripides informs us in a jesting song (*Iphigenia
among the Taurians*, 1234 ff.) how Apollo,
wishing to free himself of an unworthy competition, prevailed on Zeus to deprive the Dreams
of credibility.

Of course, the reader has long since understood
that all that has been said here is a fancy of the
bards, not binding on faith. But in general
the conviction of the prophetic significance of
remarkable dreams was very widespread, and a

' dream-book ' by Artemidorus has been preserved, large, curious, and rather important.
Even philosophy reckoned with this conviction,
interpreting the prophetic character of dreams
by the supposition that the soul of the sleeper,
unhampered by the bonds of the body, regained
its divine nature. But our own comforting
proverb, ' Dreams do deceive, in God we believe ',
was also known to the ancients : a man who had
had a disquieting dream, in the morning ' told
it to the Sun ' (a subtle act from a psychological
point of view), thus purifying himself by its
rays ; and then he prayed to Apollo that he
might fulfill the dream only in so far as it was
favourable ; but in so far as it was hostile, that he
might turn it against his enemies.

The prophetic character ascribed to the souls
of the dead at times leads men to address them,
that is, to conjure them up. . . . Greece too
had its Witches of Endor. . . . Nevertheless, in
well-ordered states they were not tolerated ;
men seized by a fatal curiosity must betake themselves to the *necromancers* of savage Epirus or
half-savage Arcadia. A reader may find in
Herodotus (v. 92) the story of how Periander,
tyrant of Corinth, conjured up the soul of his
wife Melissa, whom he had slain, or in Plutarch
(*Cimon*) another tale, how. Pausanias, king of
Sparta, summoned forth the soul of the maid of
Byzantium, whom he also had slain : they make
a deep impression.

The gods abide in a pure sphere. Entering into near relations with certain mortals beloved by them, they make them *prophets*. Thus Hesiod at the opening of his *Theogony* tells us how the Muses appeared to him on Helicon and endowed him with prophetic power ; this tale of the Boeotian bard has been justly compared with the statement of Amos in the Old Testament as to how he was made a prophet. The Bacides and the Sibyls were also regarded as prophets, and owing to the free life of Greece it is not strange that a large number of prophetic wanderers of both sexes also made their appearance and found a hearing among the people. At times the favour of the god was hereditary : thus we hear of the prophetic family of the Iamidae at Olympia. Occasionally this favour was extended to all the inhabitants of a certain city : such was the case, for example, in the city of Telmissus. To be sure, this favour might consist not so much in a native gift of prophesying as in the art of soothsaying from signs, and in such case inheritance is natural.

Yet the god could immediately bestow prophetic power, not only on a man, but on a place —this was a quite intelligible consequence of the deification of nature. Here we come to the most brilliant manifestation of ancient Greek mantic—to the oracle ; and above all, of course, to ' the common hearth of all Hellas ', the *oracle at Delphi*. On the slopes of Parnassus, at the base of two naked, perpendicular crags between which flows the Castalian stream, this spot even now overwhelms the traveller by its majestic beauty.   Here once in a sacred grove arose the temple of Apollo, surrounded by a whole forest of treasuries, statues, and other votive offerings of all sorts, a living museum not only of Greek religion but of Greek history.   Here on the appointed day—once a month or even oftener—pilgrims gathered who desired to propound questions to the god.   After a sacrifice, in an order settled by lot, they questioned the god, some by word of mouth, others in writing, but without crossing the threshold of the temple. The temple servant transferred the questions to the priest, and he bore them into the interior of the temple, to its holy of holies (*adyton*). Here on a tripod sat a maiden, the Pythia, who fell into an unconscious state, as they say, owing to vapours that issued from the earth beneath the tripod.   Her words, often disconnected, were caught up by the ' prophets ' standing near, who introduced order into them, and in solemn cases gave them a versified form : such was the answer of the god.

This practice continued from the most ancient times up to those of the Emperor Julian the Apostate, more than a thousand years : how could trickery survive so long amid the most intelligent nation of antiquity ?   Just because there was no trickery in it ; there was delusion, if you wish. Cases of distinct prophecies of the future—such as the oracles of Oedipus and of Croesus—belong to the realm of legend ; in historical times Delphi was the home of good counsel how one must act in order that the issue might be ' better ' ; this ' better ' (*ameinon*) is the general watchword of the god of Delphi. Evidently in this form the god's answer could not be confuted : even in case of ill success one could not maintain that if one had not acted by his counsel, the issue would not have been still worse. Then again, after questioning the god, a believer gained greater confidence, greater self-reliance—and confidence and self-reliance are always one more chance of success.

Let us pass to *augury* : we shall here touch on only the two most solemn methods of it, on augury from the flight of birds and from sacrifices. The foundation of the first was the belief that the gods, and Zeus in particular, abode on the heights ; the birds, especially birds of prey—it was the flight of these birds only that was the basis of augury—were most near to them, and therefore could be regarded as bearers of tidings from them. Obviously they could not be observed in all places ; the augurs had their elevations, from which they observed not only the flight of eagles, but their cries, their behaviour towards one another, towards other birds, and towards beasts (especially snakes), and the like : the phenomena which they remarked they then had to interpret.

While making a sacrifice a man is in immediate communion with the god ; one can readily understand that from the various phenomena that accompany the sacrifice he tries to divine the will of the god for whom the sacrifice was destined. These phenomena were of two sorts : some were connected with the burning of the sacrificial fire ; others with the arrangement and the form of the entrails of the beast sacrificed, especially with the design of the veins of its liver. Obviously all this had to be artificially interpreted. Augury of this sort was specially employed before a battle for the purpose of determining whether the god blessed the given moment, or whether it would be ' better ' to delay action. Therefore generals usually kept augurs with them ; and yet˜there is much food for reflection in the words of Socrates in Plato's *Laches* (198 E), that ' the augur should be under the authority of the general, and not the general under the authority of the augur '.

In the last centuries of the life of the ancient world—later than its flourishing epoch, which we are here considering—there rose and was developed a special sort of augury which eclipsed all others and which, despite all the protests of the Church, penetrated even into Christianity : this was *astrology*. As early as the third century before Christ Greece received its first fruits from Babylon through the agency of Berosus, a learned priest of Baal ; but its transformation into a

complicated system was the work of Greece
itself.

Practice makes no great demands on the intellect : the average Greek constantly availed
himself of mantic without inquiring too deeply
into its scientific premises ; he turned to the
gods with the same confidence with which
children turn to their parents for counsel.

But for thought mantic was a torturing riddle
—and not only for philosophic thought.

Of course, the gods love us and therefore
grant us cautions, whether we address them or
not : very good.   But, then, what sense is there
in the *avoidance of an evil omen* ?   I start on a
journey—and I do not bid farewell to a person
dear to me, for fear that he may weep and that
his tears may bring misfortune upon me.   I have
arrived in a carriage, and, though I am strong
and healthy, I bid my servants help me dismount,
lest—god forbid !—I should stumble and thereby
invite misfortune.   What sense is there in this ?
Perhaps god wishes to send me an omen, in
order to caution me, and I am hindering him !

It is obvious that there is no sense in this :
but take ourselves, men of modern times—why
do we avoid shaking hands with a guest across
the threshold and sitting down the thirteenth
at the table ?   Evidently a transfer of ideas has
occurred : the prophetic and cautioning omen
has turned into a magic omen.   Even a person

who believes in divination may convince himself
of this without difficulty.   He convinces himself
—and nevertheless he avoids evil omens as far as
is possible : after all such things are disagreeable.

Then, again, of course the gods know all.—
What does that mean : ' all ' ?   As to the past
we agree : Demaratus inquires of the god of
Delphi who *was* his father—that is something
that we can understand.   As to the present we
also agree : I may inquire of the same god where
my fugitive slave is at present—that is something that we can also understand.   But as to
the future ?—Let us consider.   The future certainly depends, among other factors, on the
question whether I act in this way or in that :
whoever says, ' The god possesses a knowledge
of the future ', thereby informs me, ' The god
knows how you will act '.   If so, then my acts
are predestined : consequently free will does not
exist.

On the other hand, freedom of the will is the
fundamental postulate of all Greek thinking,
of all Greek morality.   What shall we do about
it ?

The older epoch found a solution in an unfor-
mulated theory, which I have termed ' conditional fatalism '.   As a matter of fact, my will
is free, but yet it is only one of the factors
influencing the future ; then let us exclude it.
Let the god's answer be conditional: ' If Laius
begets a son, he will be killed by him ' ; ' If

Croesus passes the Halys, he will destroy a powerful kingdom.' Well then, if he does not, obviously he will not. In poetry this is very fine, but deeper and more exact thought will prove to us that this theory suits only Robinson Crusoe. For a man who dwells among other men the future depends not only on his own will, but on the wills of all those who surround him; and therefore the god's answer must be beset with such a multitude of conditions as deprive it of all value.

Hence in serious philosophy we find no trace of conditional fatalism. There the question of divination is immediately connected with the question of *divine providence*; and therefore we can easily understand why divination was recognized by the Stoa, which preached faith in providence, and was rejected not only by the school of Epicurus, but by the sceptics of the New Academy as well. The books of Cicero *On Divination*, which the Voltairianism of the eighteenth century found so important, give us an echo of this curious dispute.

Let us here consider only the positive attitude towards this question, that is, the teachings of the Stoa. If divination were impossible, the implication would be either that the gods have no knowledge of the future, or that they do not wish to reveal it to us, whether because they do not care for us, or because they regard such knowledge as useless for us. The first supposition is opposed to the idea that the deity is all-knowing, the second, to the idea that the deity is all-good, and the third is opposed to common sense.   Such is the famous trilemma of the Stoa, which later came to life again in the optimism of Leibnitz.

Let us be frank : the last two points cannot be refuted.   Not even the third.   The usual cavilling answer is that knowledge of the future is often injurious to man ; but beyond all doubt it is also often useful to him—and that is quite sufficient for the Stoa.   The one weak point in its trilemma is the first, and we already know why.   The knowledge of the future ascribed to god has as its premise predestination, and predestination excludes the freedom of the will.

. . . Does it exclude it ?   Determinism and indeterminism : the antinomy of Kant.

The Stoa did not set forth into this wilderness ; it sought a solution in another direction.   It distinguished ' fate ', ' lot ', ' chance ' ; it wrote long treatises ' on possibility '.   In vain : the ordinary aspect of things won the victory, and gradually reduced the freedom of the human will to a voluntary following of one's appointed lot.   For

Ducunt volentem fata, nolentem trahunt.

[SENECA, *Epist.* 107.]

Such is the hero of Virgil's *Aeneid*, who is funda-mentally different from the heroes of free will portrayed in ancient and modern tragedy, and

who is therefore fundamentally unintelligible
to the shallow criticism of to-day, especially
that of the Germans—Boissier is the man who
has understood him.   Stamped on his brow is
the motto that I have just cited, which casts over
him a shadow of tragic sorrow.   And this same
stamp of sorrow we find likewise on the brows
of the other great Stoics of the Empire : Seneca,
Epictetus, the Emperor Marcus Aurelius.   So it
was of necessity : whoever had glanced into the
prophetic abyss of Trophonius, the ancients were
wont to say, never laughed thereafter.

Let us bow our heads before them—and turn
with our souls towards those who, not burying
themselves in metaphysical riddles, merely felt
over them the kindly gaze of a deity full of love,
and responded to it with filial gratitude.   Such
is Theseus in the *Suppliants* of Euripides :

> Praise to the god who shaped in order's mould
> Our lives redeemed from chaos and the brute,
> First, by implanting reason, giving then
> The tongue, world-herald, to interpret speech ;
> Earth's fruit for food, for nurturing thereof
> Raindrops from heaven, to feed earth's fosterlings,
> And water her green bosom, therewithal
> Shelter from storm, and shadow from the heat,
> Sea-tracking ships, that traffic might be ours
> With fellow-men of that which each land lacks ;
> And, for invisible things or dimly seen,
> Soothsayers watch the flame, the liver's folds,
> Or from the birds divine the things to be.
>
> [*Suppliants*, 210-213 : tr. WAY.]

' In god is the truth,' is one side of the dogma
with which we are here concerned, if you choose
to call it such.   ' In truth is god,' is the other
side.   Here we shall have occasion to speak, not
of a beautiful but sterile flower which showed
itself on the tree of Greek religion, but of a
strong and flowering branch, which produced
and which still produces many magnificent
fruits.

Every art is from god and to the glory of god—
for god reveals himself in beauty.   Every *science*
is from god and to the glory of god—for god
reveals himself in truth.   The bards were the
first teachers of Greece ;   the Muse not only sent
them inspiration, but also gave them information, which they passed on to men.   If all the
rich didactic poetry of the school of Hesiod of
the eighth and the seventh centuries had been
preserved to us, I could support what I have
said by numerous immediate examples ;   but
even those mediate inferences to which I must
restrict myself are perfectly certain.   And if
the Muse herself, as we have seen, retained to
the latest times of Greece her position in the
elementary school, the fact was merely an
ontogenetic expression of her ancient phylo-
genetic rôle.

From the practice of healing connected with
the cult of Asclepius there developed the science
of medicine ;   the father of scientific medicine,
Hippocrates, sprang from a family of priests of

Asclepius, the Asclepiadae of the island of Cos ;
and this island, the centre of the cult of
Asclepius, was even in later times something in
the nature of a faculty of medicine. A side branch
of the science of the Asclepiadae was the knowledge of healing herbs, which in time developed
into pharmacology and thereby became one of
the two sources of scientific botany. The other
source of botany, that to which the science owes
its name, was the knowledge of plants fit for
grazing, which was the gift of Hermes and Apollo,
the gods of cattle-raising. Augury from the
flight of birds forced men to pay heed to their
life and habits ; thus arose ornithology, the first
branch of zoology—in this way even that sterile
flower was not completely without fruit.
Similarly the scrutiny of the entrails of sacrificial
animals, which was important in another branch
of augury, as a side issue produced anatomy,
which, although it was not the source of medicine,
nevertheless united with it and thereby transformed it from empiricism into a science.
Furthermore, the father of Greek mathematics
and of our own, Pythagoras, was in point of fact
a prophet of Apollo ; and there is a profound
propriety in the legend which informs us that
after discovering his famous proposition he
offered a hecatomb to the god who had inspired
him.

But the internal strength of every science,
which enabled it to draw the proper inference

from given premises, was the *Logos*, and this
was consecrated to Hermes, who was therefore
called Hermes-Logios. It was consecrated—
that is too mild an expression. No, if verily
' in truth is god ', then the Logos itself was a god,
was the divine son of Hermes: ' Hermetism '
recognizes him as such.   In another place I have
spoken of this phenomenon, which is in every
way worthy of attention, and have established
that the divine Logos, which became so important for Christian theology, had its origin in
Greek religion, and not in philosophy.

So all honest workers of the Logos were in a
greater or less degree prophets of god.   When
Diogenes entered on a torturing period of doubts,
he applied with filial confidence to Apollo at
Delphi.   And Apollo, understanding the state
of his soul, and alluding in his reply to the
occupation of the father of Diogenes, who had
been a money-changer at Sinope, advised him
to ' re-mint his coins '—in which counsel my
reader will easily recognize the ' transvaluation
of values ' of a philosopher of very recent
times.

Diogenes, as is well known, hearkened with all
haste to this counsel ; but in doing so he merely
followed the example of another philosopher
far more famous than himself—of him whose
caricature some persons used to call him.
Socrates had not ventured to apply to Delphi
himself ; one of his most ardent disciples did so

for him. And Apollo proclaimed Socrates the
wisest of mortals. This answer perplexed the
thinker : he had been at the other extreme from
regarding his own ignorance as wisdom. But
this ignorance had made him the pupil of every
man that he met—seeing that every man
imagined that he knew at least something.
Socrates had asked his acquaintance to share his
knowledge with him ; and together with him,
with the spade of the Logos, he had striven to dig
to its foundations—and his hands had failed
him when he saw the uselessness of his efforts.
But now, winged by the word of the god, he
began with redoubled zeal to serve the Logos ;
and when his fellow-citizens, disquieted by his
activity, wished to force him to cease from that
service, he replied : ' I cannot : that would be
disobedience to the god.' Many have read
Plato's *Apology of Socrates*, from which I take
this detail ; but have many observed what is
so clearly expressed in it : that its hero is not
merely a sage, but a prophet-sage ?

This is both a fact and a symbol : by making
Socrates an eternal disciple in the name of the
Logos and, in return for his discipleship, award-
ing him the palm of the highest wisdom, the god
repeated in one person what in more ancient
times he had done for all Hellas. Hellas likewise had regarded herself as the eternal disciple
of almost all the peoples with whom she had
come into contact by the will of fate—whereby,

let us add, she led many men into error and still
continues to do so.   And owing to this, she
became the wisest of all nations ;   she became
the mistress of the modern world.

' In truth is god '—these words, profound as
they are, nevertheless hold hidden within them
a frightful danger.   And the glory of Hellas
would be incomplete if we could not prove that
she avoided that danger.

There is but one truth : if god is in truth, then
who is in untruth ?

If we venture to reply ' the devil ', we shall
open the lips of those who excommunicate, we
shall light the pyre on which heretics are burned.
We shall justify every manifestation of *intolerance*.

We have already seen that the devil was
foreign to the Greek religion.   There was god—
and earth, ' mother ' earth, *materia ;* this Latin
word very beautifully expresses the depth of
synthesis hidden in this concept in the feeling
of the Greek.   A mother cannot be a force of the
devil.   God is good, but matter is not evil : it is
only unevenly penetrated by the goodness that
flows from god ; and we call ' evil ' only that
which is not yet sufficiently warmed by the sun of
good.

Here the situation is the same.   God is truth,
beyond a doubt ; and yet error (in the general
sense of untruth) is not the devil and cannot

be so, for there is no devil at all.   Error is merely
that field of consciousness on which the sun of
god, who is truth, does not yet sufficiently shed
its beams.

Seeing that this is the case, there is no purpose
in excommunicating and casting anathemas ;
men must cease to expel a devil who does not
exist.   Strive that the sun may conquer ; in it
all shall be made perfect.

IX

CONCLUSION

MOST of the facts cited in the present sketch are no secret for students of Greek religion ; but nevertheless that religion has here been illuminated with an entirely new and fresh light. This is due to the fundamental principle of which I spoke at the outset : we have lighted in our hearts the torch of religious feeling—and have left at home the dim rushlight of sectarianism.

But in the same measure that, when so illuminated, Greek religion has proved more beautiful and perfect, the more importunate has become the query: Why, then, did it disappear? We are wont to believe in the justice of the verdicts of history—and it was Greece which taught us to believe in it. What part in this disappearance was played by Justice, by her who shares the throne of Zeus ?

This query requires an answer, and the answer will form the ' conclusion ' of the present book.

We might reply by a request to compare the proud, free Hellenes, who in the epoch of Pericles and of Plato prayed to Athena-the-Maiden of

Phidias, and who celebrated the mysteries of Demeter at Eleusis, with those humiliated Greeks who after the lapse of several centuries accepted the religion of the cross. We might show how their gradual subjection, the loss of their political freedom, their economic exploitation, the plundering of the treasures of their religious art, and the impoverishment of their festivals gradually deprived them of that ardour of spirit which blended in a harmonious whole with their joyous religion. The right of choice presupposes in men spiritual freedom; but a man in subjection awaits the imperious voice of a master, awaits a canon that shall take a burden from him—yes, the burden of liberty.— And this answer will contain a considerable portion of the truth.

We might point out that even in their state of intellectual slavery the Greeks, the inhabitants of ancient Hellas, did not quite of their own free will allow their ancient religion to be torn from them. The teachings of St. Paul on the Areopagus did not convert the Athenians, and even in later times the descendants of Pericles and Sophocles did not readily yield to the temptation of a foreign faith. Alas, what formed the principal charm of Greek religion, its cult of visible beauty, its deification of nature, its beautiful and joyous ritual—all this was the side of it most exposed to the blows of violence. The destruction of the house of Jehovah on Zion did not injure Judaism ; the religion survived in the rolls of the Torah and the Prophets, and the synagogue successfully continued the work of the temple. But when Alaric the Goth, a Christian and a barbarian, destroyed the temple of Demeter at Eleusis ; when the hammers of fanatics demolished the prophetic revelations of Phidias, Praxiteles, and their compeers ; when the processions to Pallas on her Acropolis and the spectacles in the theatre of Dionysus were forbidden—then in truth the very soul of Greek religion weakened and withered.—And this answer will contain another portion of the truth.

And finally—this third answer is in apparent opposition to the first two, but in reality completes them—and finally, the Greek religion did not entirely vanish from the consciousness of the Christianized world : it penetrated into it, it lives in it to this day, and will live so long as Christianity itself shall live. This answer contains a third, and the most important, portion of the truth. Experts know this, but the general public does not ; and since the present book is designed particularly for that public, it behoves us to examine more closely this third answer.

Judaism is universally regarded as the stock from which Christianity grew forth : with it then we will begin.

We must not close our eyes to the great merits
—not only poetic, but moral and religious—of
the Old Testament. From an absolute point
of view it occupies a very honourable position ;
from a relative point of view it does also, if we
compare with its religion the religions of the
peoples that surrounded Israel—those Baals and
those Astartes with their human sacrifices and
their religious prostitution. But in the present
case we must not compare it with them, but with
the religion of a nation which, though it never
called itself chosen, was nevertheless—no, for
that very reason—really such. Here the result
of the comparison and the relative estimate
cannot be doubtful.

Judaism first of all did not recognize the revelation of god in beauty ; it excluded one of
the three ideals of perfection ; it rejected one of
the three sides of the sacred triangle in which for
us the eternally watchful eye of the deity reposes.
With it there also vanished the deification of
nature: the Judean [1] did not cherish filial feelings for the great mother—Earth.

Goodness and truth remained ; but even here
one must make important reservations. The
Judean's idea of good did not include a feeling
of general human brotherhood, a humanitarian
feeling : he limited his attachment to a small

[1] This translation follows the original in distinguishing the terms
Israelites (up to the time of the Babylonian captivity), *Judeans*
(from the return from captivity to the time of Hadrian), and *Jews*
(from the time of Hadrian to the present).

fraction of humanity, withdrawing in disgust
from all others, building up between himself
and them an impassable barrier in the shape of
the prohibitions of a common table, as to which
he himself admitted that Jehovah had given
them to him for the very purpose of making
difficult his communion with 'pagans'. (See
Pseudo-Aristeas, 139, 142.)

Even of his own nation, moreover, he rejected
one half, women, regarding them as unworthy of
the entire favour of Jehovah. No one who has
become acquainted with Greek religion will ever
forget the picture of the Greek priestess and
prophetess ; in this book we have been able
merely to cast a passing glance at her, and for
that matter at the priesthood in general, and yet
I hope that the names of Theano and Diotima
will not escape the reader's memory. If he
wishes to enlarge his conception, let him compare
with them the prophetess Theonoë in the *Helen*
of Euripides, the Pythia in the *Ion* of the same
author, or even the priestess of Aphrodite in
the *Rudens* of Plautus. Israel in its most ancient
times still had prophetesses such as Deborah,
but towards the end of the kingly period the
prophetesses of Israel were already busy with
'sewing pillows upon all elbows' (Ezekiel xiii. 18),
and the result of the development was the well-
known prayer of Rabbi Jehudah ben Ilai, who
openly thanked God that he had not made him
a woman. Yet one must admit that this cir-

cumstance did not in the least hamper Judaism among women during the epoch of proselytism : quite the contrary. This, however, is a riddle of another sort, one which finds its solution not in the history of religions, but in feminine psychology—and most readily in the fact that women like best not only the men but the religions that love them least.

Finally, even in his male community the Judean, in contrast to the Greek, understood the idea of good mainly in its negative sense, as a refraining from evil acts ; and as evil he regarded all that immediately or mediately, even in the most distant fashion, might offend against the Law. Thus there developed that peculiar morality of the Law, concentrated in innumerable precepts about keeping the Sabbath holy and about prohibited foods ; the Pharisee became the ideal of Jewish virtue.

There are necessary reservations also for the principle, ' god reveals himself in truth ', on the soil of Judaism. Thus, of course, God was truth for the Judean as well as for the Greek, and the Judean recognized divination and the existence of prophets. But in the first place, this principle found no corrective in the principle, ' the truth is God ' : the Judean found in his religion no spur to activity in the domain of knowledge ; for science Judaism was as fruitless as for art.—Later the Jews (not the Judeans) attained great results both in science and in art, and wrote many famous names on the tablets of progress; but this became possible for them only at the moment when, as a nation, they began to share in general human culture, and through it in Hellenism.

And in the second place, the danger from which the Greeks were protected by their organically negative attitude towards the devil, for a corresponding reason made itself felt in Judaism with terrible force : for the Judean *his* truth from the very beginning enters the confines of *intolerance*. This intolerance—let us say so at once—was the most fatal gift that Christianity received from Judaism.

And let us also say at once : When we have to deal with slavish souls, this intolerance becomes an important guarantee of success ; hereby we may complete our first answer to the question as to the decline of the Greek religion. The intolerance of the Christian apologists, which would have exposed them to ridicule in the Athens of Pericles, acted powerfully on the slavish intellects of his successors six centuries later. We may verify this by an example from the comparatively recent past. Of all the sects of the Reformation the Socinians were beyond a doubt the most enlightened and the most attractive ; as true sons of the Renaissance they inherited its tolerance as well as other qualities; and for that very reason they perished. The psychology of the matter is very simple.

' Tell me, Socinus, can I be saved if I am, let us
suppose, a Calvinist ? '—' Certainly, provided
that you are good and upright.'—' Thank you.
And now tell me, Calvin, can I be saved if I am
a Socinian ? '—' Certainly not : why did I burn
Servetus ? '—' Then I will join Calvin : that is
surer both ways.'—One must assume, I repeat,
that we are dealing with a slavish soul.

One thing more I must remark at once : the
fatal gift of intolerance, which Christianity had
received from Judaism, proved to be a two-
edged sword ; the Christians turned it against
their own masters.   Herein there is a great and
terrible lesson : all the persecutions of the Jews
that defile the history of the Christian religion
have their source in the Old Testament.   And
conversely, words of tolerance in regard to them
were spread abroad under the influence of a
revival of the ancient view of the world : I may
instance, in the epoch of the Renaissance, Reuch-
lin and his dispute with the men of Cologne ;
in the epoch of neohumanism, Lessing.   We
have an impressive picture : the anti-Semite in
his fanaticism acts, as it turns out, under the
immediate or mediate influence of Judaism ;
the humanitarian defender of the Jews, under
the immediate or mediate influence of Hellenism.

Yet a humanitarian attitude to the adherents
of a given religion does not exclude an objective
criticism of that religion.   A criticism of Judaism—brief, as is everything in this book—was

indispensable in connection with our reply to the question why the Greek religion was supplanted by the Christian religion.

During the second, and still more during the first century before Christ, Hellenism encircled with a tighter and tighter ring the land governed by Zion ; under the last Asmoneans, and above all under Herod the Great, Judea became to a considerable degree a Hellenistic kingdom. If even in Jerusalem the zealous adherents of the Law, and the morality based upon it, had to contend violently against the ever-increasing influence of the ' Hellenizers ', then what must have been the temper of the border province on the upper Jordan, ' pagan Galilee ' (' Galilee of the Gentiles ') which had only recently submitted to the authority of the Law ? Here we can do no more than ask the question : Galilee in the epoch just preceding the birth of Christ is a great riddle for us.

But it is a fact that Galilee was wedged into Hellenism still more deeply than Judea itself ; it is a fact that the appearance of Christ came at the time of the strongest influence of Hellenism on the intellects of the Judeans ; it is a fact that His teaching was a protest against Judean attachment to the letter of the Law, in the spirit of Hellenic liberty, Hellenic humanitarianism, the Hellenic filial relation to a god whom men *love*. Every man's own scientific conscience may whisper to him the conclusion to be drawn from this.

Yet at all events Galilee gravitated politically towards Jerusalem—and it was the tragic dream of the Master to gather together her children 'even as a hen gathereth her chickens under her wings'. Hence the Judeo-Christianity of the first decades both in Palestine and in the diaspora ; hence the fatal *Judaization of Christianity*, which also grafted on it a trait from which it could not free itself even in later times—*intolerance*.

Slowly, however, Judaism eliminated from its organism Christianity, which could not be reconciled with it : the Christian communities in Palestine perished, and in the diaspora the new teaching passed from the nucleus of Jewish communities to the ring of proselytes that surrounded them, and so farther and farther into that ' pagan world ' with which it was much more nearly akin. The result of this passage was the fruitful process, pregnant with consequences, the nature and meaning of which has been explained by the scientific researches of the last century—the *Hellenization of Christianity*.

To be sure, this Hellenization of Christianity advances hand in hand with the destruction of Hellenism ; the struggle of the two religions, which begins in the third century, is accompanied by frightful losses of the cultural values of humanity, at the very thought of which the heart bleeds. Amazement seizes us at the

sight of that senseless, suicidal fury with which
a people turned against all the most beautiful
and most noble creations which it had itself
fashioned from the very beginning of its existence on earth. The 'pagan' temples might
have been adapted to Christian services—the
example of the Parthenon proved this. No:
the abodes of 'devils' must be destroyed. The
fruits of the inspiration of Phidias, Praxiteles,
and other artists might have been preserved as
museum curiosities; an edict of the most
Christian Emperor Theodosius even required
this. No: the statues of 'devils' must be
demolished. This visual beauty perished; and
there perished also a whole literature that was
related to the 'pagan' worship, all the liturgi-
cal hymns, all the writings of theologians and
exegetes. The reader of even this little book
should remember that what he has read in it
rests on data derived from secular literature;
that if we had in our hands the writings of the
ancient prophets and expounders of the native
religion, our survey of it would be as much more
eloquent as an account of the history of ancient
art would be more eloquent, if our museums,
instead of late and for the most part mediocre
copies, possessed the original works of Phidias
and Praxiteles.

A simoon flew over the meadows and groves of
Hellas; Hellas grew yellow and black. Yet
it remained Hellas—and on the parched ground

gradually there began to appear new shoots of
the vegetation that had been destroyed. Despite fanatics, Christianized Greece regained the
ancient gift of its Olympus, the revelation of God
in beauty. To be sure, this beauty was very
modest; humanity had to live through a new
epoch of Daedali—but yet the seeds of the future
were saved. The deity was split into three
hypostases, in the empty heights of the heavens
the Mother of God and the saints found a dwelling—and the contrast of Christian monotheism
to ' pagan ' polytheism became a mere illusion.
The new cult began to shine with the colours
of symbolic ceremonies, which were really only
a pale recollection in comparison with the Panathenaea and Eleusinia that had gone forever—
but yet they brought joy and comfort to the soul.
The inquiring intellect began to search into the
secrets of revelation, uniting the speculation of
the Academy, the Lyceum, and the Stoa with
the fundamental theses of the new religion; and,
conducted by the Logos of ancient times, created
Christian theology.—It is true that when thinking of it we can also hardly fail to remember
excommunications and persecutions, executions
and religious wars; but Hellas is not to blame
for that. In itself the dispute of Arius and
Athanasius over the nature of Christ was just
as innocent as the dispute in earlier years
between the Lyceum and the Stoa over the
nature of the gods—as disputes there is a com-

plete analogy between them. What distinguishes them is that the Christian dispute passed from word to deed, from argument to persecution ; this is due to the unfortunate conviction that the salvation of the soul depends on the acceptance of one or the other theory, that one theory comes from God and the other from the devil. And whence that conviction arose we already know.

In truth, Hellenized Christianity, unfortunately for itself, could not rid itself of the erroneous identification of its God with the God of Abraham, could not free itself from the Old Testament, that great and remarkable book—which, however, can only gain in value in the eyes of a Christian if he ceases to regard it as a book of revelation. The blame was due to the Judeo-Christian delusion that the coming of Christ had been foretold by the prophets of the Old Testament—a delusion so thoroughly and so mercilessly overthrown by the common labour of both Jewish and Christian investigators of modern times. The medieval Church, perceiving the danger, did all that in it lay to avoid it : on the one hand, it developed the Hellenic elements of Christianity in ritual and theology, developed them successfully, at times even surpassing its model—I may instance the touching symbolism of the ringing of the evening bells, *che pare il giorno pianga, che si muore,* the majestic sounds of the organ, the meditative

beauty of aspiring vaultings, the beneficence
of charitable foundations with their quiet peace
and active faith—and on the other hand, it tried
so far as possible to make harmless the other
source of its teachings. Yet it could not expel
it altogether ; its preservation threatened mankind, sooner or later, with the *re-Judaization of
Christianity.*

This came in the sixteenth century ; its
name is—the Reformation.

For a second time the revelation of God in
beauty was set aside ; iconoclasm destroyed the
church painting of the Middle Ages, it destroyed
also the germs of its further development :
Dürer, Cranach, and Holbein found no successors in Protestant Germany. The beautiful,
symbolic ceremonies of the medieval Church
were also destroyed : against psychology, but
in the spirit of the synagogue, worship was
reduced to nothing but the word. Nature was
once more stripped of deity : there vanished
the crucifixes that adorned the crossroads and
the summits of hills, the chapels and the images
or pictures of the Mother of God and the saints,
which sanctified boundary lines and groves,
rocky grottos and the cavities of ancient trees,
and which reminded travellers of the presence
of the deity.

The neohumanism of the eighteenth century
brought in a reaction in this field as well as in
others ; its approach to antiquity inevitably

involved an approach to Hellenic Christianity as well. Orthodox Protestants even to-day cannot be reconciled to the fact that Schiller becomes a ' Catholic ' in *The Maid of Orleans* and *Mary Stuart*, Goethe a ' Catholic ' in *Faust*, particularly in the second part of the work. But there was no help for it ; the inexorable circle of evolution has been concluded, Judaized Christianity has overthrown itself in the last phase of its evolution, in the school of Harnack. It has admitted the justice of the prophetic words of Goethe : ' Gefühl ist alles.' *Religious feeling is the kernel of religion* ; the rest is but a parable.

And this consciousness should force us to regard with dignity and love a religion which gave so wide and grateful a field to the religious feeling of the faithful, which was the first of religions to recognize the revelation alike in beauty, in goodness, and in truth, and which created that sacred triangle in which for us the eternally watchful eye of the deity reposes.

INDEX

Abraham, 221.
Academus, 111, 172.
Academy, 10, 12, 181, 220 ; Middle, 172 ; New, 76, 200.
Achaean epoch, 75, 81, 82, 99.
Achaeans, 118, 135.
Acheloüs, 20.
Achilles, 24.
Acropolis, 49, 50, 57, 61, 75, 82, 85, 105, 110, 128, 129, 211.
Admetus, 43.
Aeschylus, 12, 31, 49, 57, 64 ; *Agamemnon*, 68, 77, 118, 119, 136, 142 ; *Eumenides*, 5 ; *Fragments*, 31 ; *Oresteia*, 75 ; *Prometheus*, 52 ; *Seven Against Thebes*, 33.
Africa, 30, 37.
Agamemnon, 134, 187.
Agonistics, 88, 106.
Alaric, 211.
Alastor, 142, 143.
Alcamenes, 67.
Alcibiades, 138.
Alexander the Great, 120.
Alexandria, 28, 59, 72.
Ammon, 119.
Amos, 194.
Amphictyonic Council, 114.
Amphictyony, 112-114.
Amphidromia, 92.
Amphitrite, 23.
Anatomy, 204.

Anaxagoras, 27.
Anaximander, 19.
Ancestors, spirits of, 94.
Animatism, 62.
Animism, 145.
Antenor, 77.
Anthesteria, 48, 89, 110, 145.
Apaturia, 89, 97, 101.
Aphrodite, 2, 28, 31, 42, 70, 108, 129, 136, 137, 213.
Apollo, 43, 44, 46, 55, 56, 59, 64, 66, 69, 70, 75, 76, 80, 84, 103, 114, 119, 120, 124, 125, 126, 128, 129, 135, 136, 151, 160, 172, 184, 185, 188, 192, 193, 195, 199, 204, 205, 206.
Aquinas, St Thomas, 125.
Arcadia, 21, 22, 43, 44, 64, 193.
Arcadians, 9, 10, 43.
Arcesilaüs, 172.
Architecture, 80-83.
Arcturus, 29.
Areopagus, 210.
Ares, 104, 119.
Argos, 19, 20, 104.
Aristeas, Pseudo-, 213.
Aristophanes, *Clouds*, 7, 161 ; *Frogs*, 148, 149.
Aristotle, 12, 163, 174, 176, 180, 181, 183, 185 ; *Constitution of Athens*, 34 ;